Aurelia Read Spencer Rogers

Life Sketches of Orson Spencer and others and History of Primary Work

Aurelia Read Spencer Rogers

Life Sketches of Orson Spencer and others and History of Primary Work

ISBN/EAN: 9783337326715

Printed in Europe, USA, Canada, Australia, Japan

Cover: Foto ©ninafisch / pixelio.de

More available books at **www.hansebooks.com**

Aurelia S. Rogers.

PREFACE.

THE desire to write a sketch of my own and my father's life, including the genealogy of his family, first prompted the writing of this book. My thought was, thereby to begin a chain to which other links might be added by future workers. A chain by which our family connections might be drawn closer together, and become in some degree at least, better acquainted with each other. Yet, up to this time, my father's posterity has become so numerous that it is considered best not to have their names recorded in this book. But in another book, material for which is already being gathered, our family records will be traced, where the names of those coming after may be added. In the genealogical work, here mentioned, I am being assisted by my nephew, H. B. Clawson, Jr., sister Ellen's eldest child.

Again, I have thought it proper to explain to

the people and children of the Latter-day Saints, the origin and intent of Primary work; and this explanation will be found in Part Second of this volume. For very kind and able assistance in the editing of this book, I am deeply indebted to my faithful friend and co-laborer, Sister Lula Greene Richards.

The writings of this book will probably not escape criticism; but I trust that my critics will be charitable, and consider the motives which have prompted such an undertaking by

THE AUTHOR.

DEDICATORY.

THIS book is affectionately dedicated to my children; to the descendents of Orson and Catherine Spencer; their immediate relatives and the children of the Latter-day Saints.

Our children are our jewels; we have counted well the
    cost;
May their angels ever guard them, and not one child be
    lost.

A. S. ROGERS.*

DEDICATION.

BY JOSEPHINE SPENCER.

"In lives however humble there oft gleams
Some truth or lesson—some bright light that streams
Through all the troubled seeming, and dim ways,

---

*The family name, Rogers, was originally spelled Rodgers; but for many years the d has been omitted by our branch of the family, and for this reason is not inserted in this work.

DEDICATORY.

To 'lumine earth's dark problems with its rays.
The greatest heroes are not always those
Whose names are blazoned, or whose life-page glows
With tales of martial glory, public pride,
And titled honor—; in earth's spaces wide,
And through all ages there have dwelt unsung
A multitude of souls with life chords strung
To noblest music;—uncrowned lords of earth,—
Brave men and women—kings and queens of worth—
Princes of principle—knight-errants born
To battle for the truth from earliest morn
To latest even—and whose life-deeds make
Such perfect poems as only martyr's wake.

And could these lives be written and their days,
Care-crossed, and trial-chastened—crowned with rays
Of light from victories whose struggle brought
More anguish than earth's battle-fields have wrought—
Be given that glory which gilds oft the life
That wrecks an empire, or stirs souls to strife—
The earth would ring with paeans, and heaven's bar
Thrill at the mighty jubilance afar!

The world has set false beacons for our aim—
Has set such weight on earthly power and fame
That the true value of the lives that run
In humble channels till time's hour is done,

DEDICATORY.

Glide all unnoted midst swift tides that roll
To swell the surging deep—life's mighty whole—
Whose sum is writ in Heaven's great record-book;—
Yet when time's veil is rent, and we shall look
Upon the mighty scroll with view wide-ranged,
Then shall the place of precedence be changed—
And over highest names of earth shall stand
The humblest of her noble martyr-band.

Though in the simple story of this book,
One shall in vain for pomp or prowess look.
Yet there are hearts, perchance, which viewing deep
The steadfast patience, and high faith which keep
Their purpose at the helm of life-barks frail
That float along the current of this tale—
Shall gain some help and courage from the sight
To guide their life course truer by its light.
If not for this yet shall its pages live
To serve the aim which fostered them, and give
To kindred hearts a record of past days;
Of happy childhood hours—of old home ways
Their feet oft trod together—and shall wreathe
A garland of these memories to breathe
Now, and in future years, some fragrance sweet
To old—and newer kindred—who shall greet
With praise and pleasure all the loving thought
With which the author of its pages wrought."

CONTENTS.

CHAPTER I.—Parentage and Birth of the Author...... 9
CHAPTER II.—Childhood days............................ 12
CHAPTER III.—Memories of Nauvoo...................... 22
CHAPTER IV.—Persecution and Death of Joseph and Hyrum Smith.. 31
CHAPTER V.—Uncle Hyrum's Brave Death............. 42
CHAPTER VI.—Sister Ellen, the "Little Mother."..... 47
CHAPTER VII.—Letters from Orson Spencer to his Children 52
CHAPTER VIII.—Journey across the Plains............. 76
CHAPTER IX.—Orson Spencer in England.............. 82
CHAPTER X.—Extracts from Articles and Letters...... 106
CHAPTER XI.—Father's Return........................... 120
CHAPTER XII.—Marriage and Home in Farmington. 123
CHAPTER XIII.—My Father's Last Mission—Letters to His Family.. 130
CHAPTER XIV.—Death of Elder Orson Spencer 142
CHAPTER XV.—A few Months in Salt Lake City...... 153
CHAPTER XVI.—Salmon River Tragedy—The move South.. 159
CHAPTER XVII.—The Trial of Sickness and Death— Words of Pres. Heber C. Kimball................ 163
CHAPTER XVIII.—Marriage and Death of Sister Lucy 166
CHAPTER XIX.—A Trying Ordeal—Mission of Elder Thomas Rogers to England........................ 169
CHAPTER XX.—Duty and Affection of Children— Sorrow Again.. 174

CONTENTS.

CHAPTER XXI.—Brother Howard............................ 181
CHAPTER XXII.—Brother George........................... 189
CHAPTER XXIII.—Mission to Arizona—A Romantic Incident—Face to Face with a Bear............... 194

PART SECOND.

CHAPTER I.—History of Primary Work—Letter from E. R. Snow... 205
CHAPTER II.—Primary Work Continued.................... 212
CHAPTER III.—Quarterly Meetings—Planting Beans 218
CHAPTER IV.—Sister Eliza's Work in Organizing—Louie B. Felt's Calling................................... 221
CHAPTER V.—Primary Fairs—Martial Music............. 224
CHAPTER VI.—Discouragement—Happy Result...... 230
CHAPTER VII.—Co-Laborers—Pleasant Surprises...... 234
CHAPTER VIII.—Extracts from my Journal.............. 243
CHAPTER IX.—Visits to Summit County, Utah, and to Cassia County, Idaho................................. 247
CHAPTER X.—Bible References—Another Surprise... 255
CHAPTER XI.—Members of the First Primary Association—Reflections....................................... 266
CHAPTER XII.—A Dream—Further Testimonies of Appreciation.. 276
CHAPTER XIII.—Loved Ones Gone Before.............. 283
CHAPTER XIV.—Primaries in Box Elder and Cache Stakes... 298
CHAPTER XV.—Visits to Atlanta, Georgia, and Washington, D. C... 301
CHAPTER XVI.—The White House—The Washington Monument—Council Meetings—Mount Vernon—Home Again... 312
CHAPTER XVII.—Crowning Evidences of Love........ 322
CHAPTER XVIII.—Concluding Testimonies—Tribute by Lula.. 329

LIFE SKETCHES.

CHAPTER I.

PARENTAGE AND BIRTH OF THE AUTHOR.

My father, Orson Spencer, was born on the 14th of March, 1802 in the town of West Stockbridge, Berkshire County, Massachusetts. He was the son of Daniel Spencer and Chloe Wilson Spencer; next to the youngest of eleven children and one of twins, the other twin being a girl. My grandmother not being able to take care of both the children, gave the little girl into the care of the nurse, who, while sleeping very soundly one night, laid upon the babe and caused its death.

At the age of fourteen my father had a serious sickness which nearly cost him his life. It was caused by bathing when too warm in cold water. Being an adept at running and jumping, he had been engaged in those exercises, and at that time failed to use the precaution of cooling off before entering the cold water. In that way he contracted a severe cold, which brought on typhus fever, from which he did not recover for nine months. This fever ultimately settled in his right leg, causing lameness for life.

Thus unfitted for any active pursuit, he was educated for the ministry. Proving an apt scholar, he graduated with honors, first at Union College, State of New York, in 1824; and again in the Theological College at Hamilton, New York, in 1829.

On the 13th of April, 1830, he married Catharine Curtis, who was born in Canaan Center, New York, March 21, 1811. She was the daughter of Samuel and Patience Smith Curtis, the youngest of thirteen children. After their marriage, my parents moved to the town of Deep River, in Connecticut, where my father labored as a Baptist Minister, receiving a salary which kept his family comfortably.

While living there, three children were born to them. Catharine the eldest, was named for my mother, and died when two years old. The second was named Ellen Curtis. The third child, (the writer of this humble narrative,) was named Aurelia Read, for a young lady friend of the parents. (I still have in my possession, a little red covered Testament, which she gave me as a keep-sake.)

Sometime after my birth, my parents moved into the suburbs of the town of Middlefield, Hampshire Co., Mass., my father continuing to labor in the ministry.

While we lived there, three more children were added to the family. The first of these, Catharine, was named for Catharine Read, sister of Aurelia. The fifth child was named Howard Orson. The sixth child and second son, George Boardman, was named in honor of a missionary friend. Sister Ellen wanted him named Edward, but father objected saying he would be called "Ed." He did not like nick-names, and would never allow us children to nick-name each other.

NOTE—For dates of birth of my father's children, see end of part first, this book.

CHAPTER II.

CHILDHOOD DAYS.

My earliest recollections are of living in Middlefield in a large-two story house, facing east. The ground on the north side of the house rose gradually. And when one of those terrific snow-storms, prevalent there in the winter season, came on, the snow would drift so high that we could step from the upper window out on to the frozen snow bank. Afterwards, when a thaw came, the streets would be flooded with water.

When the roads were in this condition, a man who lived at our house would take Ellen and me, one on each arm, and carry us to the school house, which was in the town, about half a mile from our home.

Children in those days were sent to school at an earlier age, I think, than they are now. For Ellen, when seven years old could "spell down" a whole school of nearly grown boys and girls.

We went to school through the week, and on Sunday the horse was hitched to the buggy, or sleigh, and we were carried to church, where we must sit very quiet during the services.

I remember having been told that God lived in Heaven, above us. So one day I went out doors and looked up into the sky, thinking I might see Him walking among the clouds. And I was quite disappointed, that He did not make Himself visible.

One thing I remember very distinctly; that although my father could not work at hard physical labor, as most men could, he would saw and split up wood, partly for exercise, as his time was mostly taken up in studying and writing. I can remember seeing the nice shed filled with wood, expressly for my mother's use. This convenience father always managed to have wherever we moved.

Children are apt to notice what "father and mother" do, thinking they are about perfect. This is, perhaps, what often causes a young man, after marriage, to tell the wife how "mother did," thinking no other way half so good. This course, however, is very unwise unless done in great kindness.

I have often thought, when remembering my father's way, if boys were taught when a load of wood is brought home, to use their spare time in sawing, splitting and piling it up in some convenient place, secure from storm, it would save many a woman much work and worry over getting a meal of victuals.

While we lived in Middlefield, I used to get up in my sleep, so I was told, and walk around the house. Sometimes I would go and sit on a bench behind the stove as if warming myself. My parents did not care to waken me, not knowing what the consequence might be; so would lead me back to bed as quietly as possible. This occasional sleep walking continued until I was twelve years old, when I was cured of it entirely; how, will be explained farther on.

Among my early recollections, one thing comes distinctly to my mind. While playing in the barn with other children, I happened to fall through an opening in the hay-loft, to the ground. Striking on my stomach, the breath was knocked out of me. I was picked up and carried to the house, where I soon recovered. But

I was petted that night in particular and placed in baby's high chair at the supper table. That fall might have been partly the cause of my stomach trouble in later years.

In the year 1840, my uncle, Daniel Spencer, came from West Stockbridge, which was about one day's journey, to make us a visit, and preach Mormonism, or, more properly speaking, the true gospel of salvation, which he had received, and unto which he had been baptized. Like every true Latter-day Saint, he wanted others to know about it, as well as himself.

In talking with my father and mother, he must have told them of the youthful Prophet, Joseph Smith, of his seeing the Father and the Son in vision; of the Angel Moroni, who told him where he was to find the records from which the Book of Mormon was translated; and many other things which agreed with the doctrines of Christ in former days.

My parents could not reject the Truth, although father held back a little at first perhaps for the sake of argument. They sat up late every night during the few days my uncle stayed, conversing upon the principles of this new doctrine which was to make such a change in their future lives; when one evening my mother said looking at my father, "Orson, you know this is true!" He felt to acknowledge it, and they both shed tears, feeling the influence of the Holy Spirit in their midst. Soon after, they were both baptized.

The next consideration was, how to gather with the Saints, who were then settling in Nauvoo, Illinois. Father must give up his means of making a livelihood, meet the scorn and derision of old friends, etc. But once convinced that he was right, nothing could turn him from his purpose.

He accordingly took steps to dispose of his private property, in which was a library of choice books. He settled up all business accounts, and in the Spring of 1841, started for West Stockbridge, the place of his birth, and where his parents still lived.

While stopping at Grandfather Spencer's, Ellen and I went one day with some little girls to visit their school, which was about a mile off.

It seemed that on this day our parents had concluded to go to Uncle Hyrum Spencer's, four miles farther on their journey. They waited until after the usual hour for school to close, then went without us, leaving word that we should be sent on in the morning. We had been persuaded to stop and play by the way, coming from school. After reaching home, however, and finding that we were left, no words can describe my feelings. Grandmother could not make me understand that we were to go to our parents in the morning, for I supposed that they had gone out west, the place they had told us so much about; so I cried as if my heart would break, and nothing could pacify nor quiet me, until I fell asleep through exhaustion. Ellen being older and having more judgment, did not feel so badly; but I learned a lesson from that experience, which was, to go straight home from school. We were sent to my uncle's the next day, where my parents stayed for a few months, preparing for their journey to Nauvoo.

Uncle Hyrum had also joined the Church. He

had a large family, mostly girls; the eldest of whom took charge of the house, as his wife had died some time previous.

I hope my readers will bear with me, in relating some incidents of my younger days, which although they may seem of little interest to others, made lasting impressions on my mind.

There is a saying, that "the boy is the father of the man," then why not "the girl, the mother of the woman?" It is certain that children often show out in childhood what occupation would be most natural for them to follow when they come to years of maturity.

I think my forte would be to teach children, if I could have been educated for it; for while staying at Uncle Hyrum's, I used to go into his wood shed, which was a little way from the house, and play school, having sticks of wood for my scholars.

I would arrange them in classes, then get my rod of correction and commence going through the exercises the best I knew how.

On one of these occasions, while busily engaged drilling my pupils, I happened to look through an opening in the boards, at the back of the shed; when, O, horror! I saw my cousin Charles standing close to the corner, listening to my oratory, and ready to burst with laughter. He did not know that he had been seen, but school was dismissed rather suddenly, and I ran for the house.

Canaan Center, my mother's birth place, was only a few miles from West Stockbridge; she therefore had the opportunity of visiting her relatives, the most of whom lived in the neighborhood of Canaan. And a happy reunion it was. All that were left at the old homestead, were my Grandfather and Grandmother Curtis, and Aunt Esther who took care of them. She was their eldest child, but had not married on account of some disappointment in her youth. She loved my mother, as did all the rest of the family, and they made everything of her children; so much so, that Aunt Esther insisted on my sister Catharine and myself living with her while we were in Canaan. But Catharine used to get homesick, and only stayed part of the time. Ellen lived with Aunt Lucy, whose home was in Chatham, N. Y., about five miles from Canaan. This lightened the labor of my parents, and gave them a better chance to prepare for their journey. I was sent to school, and when Catharine was there she went with me. We never forgot the quaint little bonnets Aunt Esther made for us, to save our others. The peculiar cut of these bonnets we did not like; yet it was very kind of her to make them, and she little thought of their not being appreciated. But when we would get nearly to the school house we would take them off and put them under our arms till we got into the entry, then hang them up.

Grandfather Curtis was a tanner by trade, yet carried on farming at the same time. The tannery was just across the road from the house; well do I remember walking around the vats, and the fear I had of falling in. Also when the dinner hour arrived, how my aunt would go out on the porch or stoop as they called it and blow the horn for the men to come in from the field to dinner.

I will relate an incident which occurred while we were in Canaan, to show the power of imagination. One evening Aunt Esther happened to see me taking a drink of water, and said, "You should always look into the water before drinking, for there might be snakes or bugs in it." If she had only told me before, it would have saved us both a great deal of trouble; for I imagined directly that I had swallowed a snake, and could even feel it in my throat. Therefore aunt was kept up half the night working with and trying to convince me that nothing was there, it was only my imagination.

It had been decided in the council of the Spencer brothers, that my father should go to Nauvoo first and look out places to locate; while my uncles should stay until they could sell their property; which they did, and emigrated the next year. Strange to relate, not one of my mother's relatives ever joined the Church, and they felt quite bitter toward my father for taking their beloved one away, fearing they might never see her again; and so it was proved, although father visited them afterward.

CHAPTER III.

MEMORIES OF NAUVOO.

At length the time arrived when we were to leave the home of our childhood, and cast our lot with the Latter-Day Saints.

Father hired a team which carried us to Albany; then we went on a canal-boat to Buffalo; from Buffalo to Chicago on a steam-boat; then teams again until we reached Nauvoo.

This city was situated in a bend of the Mississippi River, which bordered the west and south sides. The land extending eastward from the river was quite level for about half a mile; then arose a bench of land, which again was pretty much on a level for miles around. This was the site of Nauvoo City. After arriving in Nauvoo father rented an unfurnished room of Mrs. Mercy Thompson, sister-in-law to Brother Hyrum Smith. This house was within a few blocks of the river, in the southern part of the city on the flat or bottom land. While staying there another little sister came to us, who was called Lucy. The Prophet Joseph Smith, who lived close by, often came in, and when he saw the baby, he exclaimed, "Oh, what a little black head!" for she had so much hair; then he laid his hand upon her head and blessed her.

The Temple was built upon the hill, facing west. A little northeast of the Temple was a public square, which at the time of our arrival was mostly covered with trees and shrubbery. On the north side of this square was our home for a few years, father having bought a lot there and built a brick house, one story and a half high with one room below and two above. He also engaged lots on the east side of the square for his brothers Daniel and Hyrum. Among our neighbors were Brother James Hendricks and family; he had been wounded by the mob in Missouri and was crippled so that he could not dress himself without assistance. For more than thirty years Brother Hendricks lived on in that condition—a living martyr for the sake of his religion.

In the second house east of us, lived Sister

Warren Smith, one of the heroines of the Haun's Mill massacre, where her husband and one son were slain, and another son was frightfully wounded. Sisters Hendricks and Smith were dear friends of my mother; in fact she had many friends, and every one was very kind to us.

One thing which seemed very odd to me was the queer talk of some of the children, and no doubt our language was just as strange to them. We were regular Yankees, and used to say "stun" for stone; while they being southerners would say, "I reckon", and, "quit that" instead of "stop that." In calling the cows they would say, "sook bossy;" and what we called "hasty pudding," they called "mush;" It took me years to get used to the word mush, and even now it sounds out of place.

In the fall of 1842, father added two rooms to the back of our house, into which we moved, using the front part for a store, which he attended to himself; he had no salary now to depend upon, therefore had to manage as best he could to make a living.

In the meantime, my uncles had emigrated and were installed in their new homes.

Father and mother went over to Uncle Hyrum's one evening, to spend an hour or two, leaving Ellen and myself home to look after the younger children. They had not been gone long, when we heard the front door open and some one come in. Ellen and Howard went to the door that led to the store, opened it and peeping into the room which was quite dark, asked, who was there. No one answered. There could have been seen some scared children then, I can tell you.

I was rocking the cradle by the stove and speechless with fear. The breathless silence was at length broken by one of our little neighbors coming out from behind the counter and making herself known, laughing heartily at our expense. But, to tell the truth, it was no laughing matter; for according to my way of thinking, scaring children is one of the worst things in the world.

I have seen mothers try to enforce obedience, by telling their little ones, "the black man would get them," or the "Indians would carry them off," if they did not mind; so that when they saw an Indian they were afraid for their lives. I always deeply deplore such things as serious mistakes.

Father only kept the store through the winter months, as he had other business to attend to in the spring, having been elected Alderman of the City. He sold his stock of goods which was not very extensive, and we moved back into the front part of the house; after that father taught school in the larger of the rooms just vacated. The school only occupied a portion of his time, enabling him to attend to his public duties as well. In this school I became acquainted with Mary Ann Stearns, stepdaughter to Parley P. Pratt. Brother Pratt had just returned with his family, from a mission to Europe. I also formed the acquaintance of Ellen Pratt, daughter of Addison Pratt. Ellen's father at that time was on a five years' mission to the Sandwich Islands. I mention these girls, as we became very dear friends, which friendship has remained up to the present time. Soon after that my father was sent on a short mission to the Eastern States during the time of which he visited my mother's relatives. The most of them were friendly, but one aunt would not receive him, and shut the door in his face.

Upon his return home, he brought Grandfather and Grandmother Spencer with him. They lived in our house, and died within a year of each other, at the ages of eighty-three and eighty four years.

It was quite common in those days for old people to smoke, and my grandmother indulged in this habit; she would often ask me to light her pipe for her; in doing so I learned to smoke and liked it so much that whenever I saw anyone smoking, I had a craving desire to take a few whiffs myself. This was innocently indulged in at intervals, for a number of years, until at length I was awakened to a sense of the danger of the habit.

There was a monitor within that told me it was wrong, and what it would lead to if persisted in; I should be, if I lived, an old lady smoker. This thought disgusted me, for I never did like to see women smoke, or men either as for that matter, so the habit was broken off entirely, although it was hard for me to drop it.

I mention this because at present I am a teacher in the Primary Associations and desire in any way I can to discourage the use of tobacco with its attendant evils. My experience in regard to the habit, with the will power it took to overcome it was quite a lesson to me.

My mother's parents lived until the year 1851, and died within a few months of each other, in their home at Canaan. Grandmother Curtis passed away in April at the advanced age of eighty-four years. My grandfather lingered until June, when he died being eighty-seven years old. They had lived together in wedlock sixty-four years.

In the meantime the Saints were moving into Nauvoo from all directions, which caused the city to spring up like magic. Stores were being erected, printing offices established, and all kinds of business necessary for the welfare of a community going on. The Temple was also being built. A music hall had been put up, about a block away from us, which was used in the day time for school purposes, and in the evenings for concerts, social gatherings, etc.

One night when there was to be a concert, Mary A. Pratt, (as we called her,) Ellen Pratt and myself were going to the house of the former to spend the evening.

When opposite the hall we saw Brother Pratt in company with two ladies coming to the concert. Mary Ann said, "Let us follow on behind father and perhaps we can get in with them." Arriving at the door, we had to go single file, each holding on to the other's dress, for fear of being separated in the crowd. As soon as Brother Pratt stepped inside the door, Mary Ann attempted to follow; but the doorkeeper stopped her and asked who she was; she said, "I am Parley Pratt's daughter," and passed in. Ellen said, "I am her cousin," (meaning Mary A.) But when it came my turn, I did not know what to say as I had not thought of an answer. So, afraid of being left out, I said, "I am some relation, I don't know what." The door keeper smiled, but let me in. We walked on behind Brother Pratt up to the front seat when he, happening to see us, got us a seat behind him.

I remember Brother Edmund Elsworth singing, "The Indian Hunter," and we enjoyed the exercises all through.

When I went home and told father and mother of my adventure, they laughed heartily at my not knowing any relationship to Brother Pratt; but warned me against ever using unfair means, for the sake of a little amusement.

Those were happy days, and I love to dwell upon them, for the change came too soon. Then we had parents to love and care for us, and help us with our lessons while going to school. Father would some times have a good romp with us in the evening, or would tell us some very interesting story. Mother being a sweet singer, would sing snatches of a hymn, or some of her old songs.

One thing can be said of my parents, I never heard them say a cross word to each other; they tried as much as possible to make their home pleasant and happy.

CHAPTER IV.

PERSECUTION AND DEATH OF JOSEPH AND HYRUM SMITH.

The Temple on Fire—Death and Obituary of the Author's Mother.

It is not worth while repeating history here. It is generally known that our enemies, seeing the prosperity of the Saints, began to hunt up excuses for serving writs on the leading members of the Church; and that this was the cause of some of the brethren going to prison, while others hid themselves to keep out of their enemies' way, similar to what they have been doing of late years, with this difference, polygamy was not the offence at that time, but hatred toward the Prophet Joseph because of the religion the Lord had revealed to him. This persecution lasted until the massacre of Joseph and Hyrum Smith, after which there was comparative peace for over a year. Well do I remember the morning after the martyrdom of those noble men. A gloom was cast over the whole city of Nauvoo; men women and children wept for their departed Prophet and Patriarch. I witnessed the long procession that followed the bodies of our beloved Leaders, as they were taken to Joseph's mansion, where they laid in state until the people could take a last look at them, and say farewell. My father lifted me through one of the windows of the mansion, as the door-ways were thronged with people, when after viewing the bodies I was passed back again and taken home.

During the before mentioned time of peace, the upper rooms of the Temple were finished, and were used for attending to the ordinances of the Church including baptism for the dead. My parents spent part of their time in assisting to carry no this work.

At one time, through oversight or carelessness, a fire started from one of these upper rooms and the blaze was soon through the roof. The cry of "fire!" was heard, men were seen on top of the building swinging their hats for assistance; the people turned out in mass, even women and children ran with buckets. Wells close by were nearly drained, and teams were sent to the river for water. I with the rest ran with a pail and gave it to some one to use; in doing so, I went up the steps of the Temple to the first landing. On each side of this landing were winding stairs which led from one story to another until the top of the building was reached. Rows of men were stationed on these stairs, to pass the buckets full of water up on one side, then pass them back empty on the other side. This was continued until the fire was put out, for it seemed that it could not withstand such a united effort.

Child as I was, I could not help noticing the order that prevailed and the calmness of the men that superintended the work.

In after years, that beautiful structure was burned down by incendiary; the stones were hauled away, and at present, not a trace of it can be seen. The ground where it stood has been converted into a vineyard.

In July, 1844, my mother had a little girl born, who was named Chloe. She died of whooping cough when thirteen months old.

Our enemies not being satisfied with what they had already done, were determined that the Saints should leave Nauvoo. And in the winter of 1845-46 my parents, in company with many others, began to make preparations to move.

Corn was parched and ground; and rusk was made of light bread, by putting it into a moderate oven, and letting it remain until it was thoroughly dried and toasted a light brown. This was put into sacks and packed away, to be pounded in morters when needed. Bread so prepared will keep good any length of time, almost, if not exposed to the damp, and is very wholesome and palatable with milk, as we used to eat it. Many crusts and crumbs which are now thrown away might be preserved in the same manner.

Our clothes were packed and, with a few other necessaries, we started for the west about the middle of February. Going to the Mississippi River in the evening, we waited our turn to cross over, as the ferry boat was running night and day.

My mother had scarcely recovered from a spell

of sickness, which followed the death of little Chloe, and was illy prepared to stand the cold weather and rough roads we had to travel over in the fore part of the journey. She therefore gradually sank from the effects of a severe cold and soon died. As we had only traveled a distance of thirty miles, her body was taken back to Nauvoo and buried. I will here insert her Obituary copied from Spencer's Letters, first edition:

Catherine Curtis Spencer, died on the 12th of March, 1846, at Indian creek, near Keosaqua, Iowa Territory, at the age of thirty-five years, wanting nine days.

In one month from the time of her departure from Illinois to the wilderness, she fell a victim to the cares and hardships of persecution. The youngest daughter of a numerous family, brought up in affluence and nurtured with fondness and peculiar care as the favorite of her father's house; her slender, yet healthy frame, could not withstand the inclemency of the winter season, (the thermometer below zero for ten days.) The change from the warm rooms of brick and plastered walls, to that of mere canvass ceiling and roof, floored with snow and icy earth, was too much for her fragile form to endure. When, through unforeseen hindrances in travelling, there was no place where sleep could visit, or food suited to the demands of nature be administered to her or her six little children from the age of thirteen and under, she would cheer her little innocents with the songs of Zion. The melody of her rare voice, like the harmony and confluence of many virtues in her mind, contributed on that memorable epoch of the Church, to render her the glory of her husband, and the solace and joy of her children. When asked if she would go to her distant friends that were not in the Church who had proffered comfort and abundance to her and her children, she would reply, "No, if they will withhold from me the supplies they readily granted to my other sisters and brothers, because I adhere to the Saints, let them. I would rather abide with the Church, in poverty even in the wilderness, without their aid, than go to my unbelieving father's house, and have all that he possesses." Under the influence of a severe cold, she gradually wasted away, telling her children, from time to time, how she wanted them to live and conduct themselves, when they should become motherless, and pilgrims in a strange land. To her companion she would sometimes say, "I think you will have to give me up and let me go." As her little ones would often inquire at the door of the wagon, "How is ma? is she any better?" she would turn to her husband, who sat by her side endeavoring to keep the severities of rain and cold from her with, "Oh, you dear little children, how I do hope you may fall into kind hands when I am gone!" A night or two before she died, she said to her husband, with unwonted animation, "A heavenly messenger has appeared to me to-night, and told me that I had done and suffered enough, and that he had now come to convey me to a mansion of gold."

Soon after, she said she wished her husband to call the children and other friends to her bedside, that she might give them a parting kiss; which being done, she said to her companion,

"I love you more than ever, but you must let me go. I only want to live for your sake, and that of our children." When asked if she had anything to say to her father's family, she replied emphatically, "Charge them to obey the gospel."

The rain continued so incessantly for many days and nights, that it was impossible to keep her bedding dry or comfortable, and, for the first time, she uttered the desire to be in a house. The request might have moved a heart of adamant. Immediately a man by the name of Barnes, living not far from the camp, consented to have her brought to his house, where she died in peace, with a smile upon her countenance, and a cordial pressure of her husband's hand.

Many tributes to her memory, from the Twelve and other distinguished friends, expressive of her worth and the amiableness of her life, have been communicated to the writer, which conjugal relationship forbids him to insert, but which are still a comfort to the bereaved in his pilgrimage through mortality.

Though prepossessing in her manner, her

confiding and generous mind always made permament the friendship that she once obtained. Her unceasingly affectionate and dutiful bearing to her husband, and her matronly diligence in infusing the purest and loftiest virtues into the minds of her children, not only exemplified the beautiful order of heaven, but made the domestic circle the greatest paradise of earth. Said a member of the High Council after her death, one who had often observed her in the Temple of the Lord, where she loved to linger and feast on the joys of that holy place, "I never saw a countenance more inexpressibly serene and heavenly, than hers."

> O! she was young who won my yielding heart;
> No power of genius, nor the pencils' art
> Could half the beauties of her mind portray,
> E'en when inspired; and how can this my lay?
> Two eyes that spoke what language ne'er can do,
> Soft as twin violets, moist with early dew.
>
> In sylph-like symmetry her form combin'd
> To prove the fond endearment of the mind,
> While on her brow benevolence and love
> Sat meekly, like two emblems from above;
> And every thought that had creation there,
> But made her face still more divinely fair.

Her remains were conveyed to the city of Nauvoo, and there, after a few neighbors had wept and sung, "Come to me; will ye come to the Saint that have died," and expressed their condolence to the deeply affected husband, buried in the solitude of the night, by the side of her youngest child, that had died near six months before.

The writer does not mourn for his dead as those without hope, knowing they are taken from many evils to come.

He desires to dedicate the above faint sketch to his children, now in the wilderness, for the testimony of Jesus, lest time should obliterate from their young and tender minds the recollections of their mother's person and some of her virtues; thereby would he perpetuate the memory of the just. He desires the prayers of all Saints for himself and his children; and may the blessing of Almighty God rest upon all who love our Lord Jesus Christ, in sincerity.

At the time my mother was moved into a house, my brother George was ill, having taken a severe cold which caused a gathering in his head and it was thought best not to leave him in camp.

Ellen having to see after the other children and the tent work (as we were then living in a tent,) it fell to my lot to be nurse, so I went along to take care of George, and was with ma when she died.

This was my first great sorrow. We missed her very much, but did not fully realize our loss until afterwards, for father seemed to take the place of both parents, looking after and caring for us faithfully.

The journey was continued as soon as the weather would permit. The company traveled on until they came to Garden Grove, where they stopped a few weeks to rest and recruit their teams, also stopped at Mount Pisgah and Council Bluffs.

CHAPTER V.

UNCLE HYRUM'S BRAVE DEATH.

While a portion of the Saints were camped at Garden Grove, my Uncle Hyrum Spencer and Uncle Daniel's son Claudius V. went back to Nauvoo to try to sell the valuable farms of the Spencer brothers. While returning Uncle Hyrum died before reaching camp, and was buried at Mount Pisgah. When we arrived at Council Bluffs, Sister Daniel Hendricks and Cousin Mary, one of Uncle Hyrum's daughters also died. These sad losses cast a gloom over the whole camp.

As very little is known in history about Uncle Hyrum, on account of his early death, I feel that a few words in regard to his character are due. The following are extracts from an article published in the Deseret News some years ago.

"Hyrum Spencer was a man of large stature and great physical power; and as void of fear as men are made. In 1838 a marvelous vision was given him, in which was shown the Southern Rebellion, and other troubles that were to come; with which manifestation he received an assurance of the truth of the Latter-day work, of which, from that time, he was enabled to testify. He embraced the gospel and moved to Nauvoo.

The day that Joseph and Hyrum Smith were martyred he was on his farm six miles east of Nauvoo, and was so influenced that he could not work; and he three times saddled his horse to go to Carthage, but rebuked himself for nervousness. He was among the first in that memorable exodus of the winter of 1836.

At the time he left the camp at Garden Grove the weather was very unfavorable. He rode fourteen days on horseback through that, then wilderness country, and not one twenty-four hours but what it rained. Arriving in Nauvoo he disposed of one farm for a hundred and ten head of cattle, and some wagons, to a citizen at Alton. A mob resident of Nauvoo hearing this, procured writs of attachment to the stock, until the second mob could arrive in Nauvoo, and give him a confiscation benefit, although at the time this man, Tod, owed the Spencers seventeen hundred dollars. Here was an issue which with the large families of the three brothers in the wilderness, plundered and measurably destitute, required tact and nerve. Through an honorable Gentile, Tod was made to believe that on a certain day the stock would cross the Mississippi at Hannibal, forty miles south of Nauvoo, and he was there with sheriff and posse.

That same day the stock crossed sixty miles above Nauvoo, and it was a race (from that to the first Mormon camp) of what might be starvation and nakedness for the women and children in the wilderness, or comparative comfort.

Six days and a half, and six nights, in the heat and flies of early August, were these cattle driven and guarded by him, and his nephew Claudius, with only six hours sleep, except on horseback. The strain was too much; he rode until 4 o'clock on the afternoon of his death, when his nephew seeing him reel, rode to his side asking him what was the matter. The reply was, "Not much, only I cannot last through; help me down and I will die here."

That night at 11 o'clock his labors were ended and he lay, with the peaceful smile of a child, a few feet from the trail, with only one relative to hear his last words, to witness the heroism of a voluntary martyr's death.

There was not a groan or a murmur, "Say to my family, live and die with this work. Take Daniel's (his brother's) council." These were among his last words.

He left eight children by the wife of his youth, and two by his then living wife, formerly Miss Emily Thompson, whom he married in Nauvoo.

The two sons of Uncle Hyrum's now living, are Charles and Hyrum Sheron Spencer. The latter is now Bishop of Pleasant Green, Salt Lake County.

After Uncle Hyrum died, two or three men from a camp near by assisted Claudius in preparing for the burial. This was done by taking some boards from a wagon-box and forming a rude coffin, in which he was taken to Mount Pisgah, and interred in the burial ground of the Saints.

Cousin Claudius managed himself to drive the cattle on, the remainder of the distance to the camp of the Saints. The fatigue, exposure and great strain of nerves which Claudius had endured was followed by a long and severe illness.

My Uncle Daniel Spencer, being among the pioneers of Utah, held several important positions of public trust. For a number of years he presided over the Salt Lake Stake of Zion. At his death, he left a large family. One of his daughters is the well known authoress, Josephine Spencer.

At Council Bluffs, I remember hearing of the call for the Mormon Battalion, to be made up of 500 of our most able bodied men, who were to march as soldiers to Mexico. President Young talked of it to the people in the bowery where our meetings were held. I saw the Battalion making preparations to march, and knew that some of our dear friends were in deep sorrow over the long separation, with increased trials and hardships, which those preparations meant.

※ ※ ※

CHAPTER VI.

SISTER ELLEN, THE "LITTLE MOTHER."

Before leaving Nauvoo, father had been called to go on a mission to England to edit the Millennial Star; but on account of the persecutions his departure had been postponed.

While at the Bluffs he was notified to be in readiness to start late in the fall. He therefore made arrangements to fill the appointment and went with us across the Missouri River to Winter Quarters, where he put up a log cabin, into which we moved before it was finished there being no floor nor door. Soon after a door was put in, but the floor, which was made of hewed logs, was not laid until the next spring.

Catharine and I were just recovering from a

spell of sickness when our father bade us farewell and started on a three years' mission, leaving us in charge of a good man and his wife by the names of James and Mary Bullock, who looked after our interest the same as their own. They also had a family of children.

The door of Brother Bullock's cabin faced our's and was only a few feet from it, so if anything went wrong they could hear us. We kept house by ourselves, Ellen acting the part of a little mother. She had just turned fourteen, and was small of her age, but had the judgment of one older. It was well for us that we had been taught to knit and sew, for we had our own clothes to mend and look after. A lady by the name of Jane Dudson, who lived across the street from us, used to cut out our dresses and then we helped to make them. From her I took my first lessons in dress cutting, which were gained by observation, and were of great use to me afterwards.

We got through the first part of the winter pretty well, as father had provided for our wants, having left us with eight cows and one horse; the horse was to be sold for provisions. We went to school to Sister Addison Pratt, (mother of Ellen Pratt) who felt obliged to do something to earn a livelihood for herself and four daughters. She was an excellent lady and we spent most of our spare time at her house.

When the weather was cold or stormy so we could not go out, the game of mumble-peg was introduced, which was all the rage among the children at that time. This we used to play on our dirt floor, which rather marred its smoothness but afforded us considerable amusement. In the evening Brother Bullock's children sometimes came in, when we would have a spelling school, or sit around the fire telling riddles and stories until bed time.

It was while living in our floorless log cabin that I was cured of walking in my sleep. We had two beds in the room, while our clothes and other goods were piled up in boxes. On the top of one of these boxes was placed a writing desk that was not very solid; in one of my midnight rambles, I happened to knock this desk off its resting place to the floor; it fell with such a crash that the noise awakened me. I was so bewildered that I could not find my way to the bed. Ellen's voice which sounded in the distance was no guide for me, for I went straight for the door, and she had to get up and lead me back to bed. I not only had a good scare, but was never known to get up in my sleep afterwards.

The winter finally passed as all winters do, and every one felt to welcome the coming of spring. There had been considerable sickness during the cold months; a disease called Scurvy had come among us, and was the cause of many a loved one being laid away in the grave.

The wife of Brother Archibald Hill was one of the victims. Brother Bullock and wife parted with two of their children, Genette and Isabel. Our family had escaped having this horrible disease but in the spring we all took the measles, myself being the first to come down with it.

The winter having been uncommon in its severity, our horse and all our cows but one had died, therefore we had no milk nor butter; our provisions had also nearly given out, so that in the spring and summer following, we really suffered for something to eat; part of the time having nothing but corn-meal, which was stirred up with water and baked on a griddle. Many a night I have gone to bed without supper having to wait until I was hungry enough to eat our poor fare. Many others as well as ourselves had very little to eat, and those who did fare better, knew nothing of our destitute condition. Some months after, Apostle Wilford Woodruff, hearing about our circumstances visited us, and relieved our wants for the time being. The Saints had to send to a place called St. Joseph, which was some miles below Winter Quarters, for provisions that consisted mainly of corn-meal and pork. There was no need of our family suffering for food, if the money father sent us had been received; but although the money failed to reach us, the letters received from our dear parent were a great comfort to us; some of which I will copy, showing the love and anxiety he had for his children.

CHAPTER VII.

LETTERS FROM ORSON SPENCER TO HIS CHILDREN.

NOTE—These letters do not follow one after another in regular succession as they were written and received; although, for convenience, they are numbered i, ii, iii, etc.

LETTER I.

THIS letter was written before my father had received any word from us, and is copied partly to show the condition of the people in Europe at that time.

STAR OFFICE, LIVERPOOL, APR. 17, 1847.

"MY DEAR CHILDREN:—In the midst of the bustle and throng of business, that at this time is greater even than usual, I snatch a passing moment, to write to you. I did not know until just now that Brother Candland would go to America quite so soon. I am constrained to write to President Young, informing him of the state of things in this country. The spiritual prospect of the saints in this country is good. The saints abound in faith and hope and an earnest desire to emigrate to America. In fact their temporal prospects are alarming if the great God were not their friend and support. But they are mostly contented and obedient to counsel, and I feel anxious to see them gathered and safely garnered in the land of Zion. I see men, women and children standing and sometimes sitting in the streets, bare-footed and bare-headed and crying for food; and they will often follow me eight or ten rods begging and praying for food. Ninety thousand people have come from Ireland to this city of Liverpool alone, to get food and employment. The multitudes that die from starvation are so numerous in places in Ireland that they are not even buried at all, but straw and grass are thrown over them and they rot above ground. More factories are stopping every day, and more and more people are thrown out of employment, and emigration is so great that there are not ships enough to take the emigrants. Freight and passage are very high and rising. Universal fear and consternation pervade England, Ireland, Scotland and France, and many other parts of Europe. They expect some dreadful calamities are coming on the nations of the earth. The cloudy tempest darkens every day and threatens soon to spend its desolating power upon all flesh save those who are hid in the mountains in cities of refuge till the indignation be passed over. There are some in high places that are so stupified with gluttony, sensuality and the love of oppression that they have not sense enough to fear. But the great body of the people are full of fearful anxiety. I am glad my children and friends are thus far removed to the wilderness. You may and must probably pass through troubled and straitened circumstances, and scarcely be saved, but fear not nor be dismayed, for the God of Israel is your God and will strengthen and preserve you, if your faith fail not. Now my beloved children, love one another and strive to please each other and don't mind little offences, but forgive and bear with each other's faults; pray often and be not angry or contentious with anybody. I know you will economize, to live in the cheapest way you can. And I say to you again and again, strive to preserve your health in the way I have always recommended. When you are not well fast and eat light food; wear flannel and warm clothes in all seasons as much as possible. Wash your bodies often in pure water, and comb your heads, that from the head to the feet you may be clean and healthy. Go to school as much as you can, all of you, in your present circumstances. Strive to have the good will of all around you. Trust to the counsel of those who are set over you in the Lord. I have not received a syllable from your pen since I left your cabin. How much I want you to tell me in your own simple, plain way, all about your condition and feelings, and how the younger children behave themselves.

"My health and strength are so good that I am well able to accomplish more labor than I have been in any time for twenty years previous. My mind is clear and ready for the multiplied duties and cares that rest upon me. I find the 'Lord God is a sun and shield.' He is wisdom and salvation to me the very moment I need it. I say this that you may learn to trust in Him for health, food and wisdom, and all things at all times.

"There is no lack to them that trust in God.

"Finally, may the God of all consolation keep you all in health and prosperity, both temporal and spiritual, unto everlasting life and blessedness, is the prayer of

> Your Affectionate Father,
> ORSON SPENCER."

In the same month that the above letter was written, my father married a lady by the name of Martha Knight, of Lancaster, England; and some wedding cake was sent to us with the next letter.

LETTER II.

"LIVERPOOL ENG., AUG. 9th, 1847.

"DEARLY BELOVED CHILDREN: The last and only letter which I have had from you, was dated Feb. 1st. I have looked wishfully, but in vain for letters from you. Perhaps you think that you have not much to write, and therefore delay.

But be assured that I would gladly pay postage fourfold for the simple knowledge that you are well, as often as once a month. But I have no doubt you can find enough to write about, even such things as you would tell me about if I were there. You will perceive that I know nothing from you, of what you have received from me, either in money or clothing. Indeed I am pained to think that I cannot hear from your own pen, what has been, and now is your condition, but I must be content. Elder Hyde wrote me the 30th of May, that he had been to see you and that you were all well. This gave me great happiness indeed. But he said you had seen rather straitened circumstances, which made me weep with sorrow.

"But I knew that you were suffering for Christ's sake, which gave me some comfort. But still I thought of your tender and parentless condition, and could but earnestly entreat my Heavenly Father to preserve and bless you. I know you have the best of friends in Brother and Sister Bullock, who will spare no pains for your comfort. And I trust I shall never forget them, either in word or deed. I fear that Brother —— did not pay you the fifty dollars that I sent by him. I trust you will get five sovereigns promised by Sister Harker on her arrival. I also sent twelve sovereigns by Elder L. N. Seavil, five or six of which I told him he might expend for groceries in St. Louis for you. I also sent six sovereigns by Elder Jacobs. These brethren may reach you the last of September. I shall send you more the first opportunity, which may be by Brother Martin. If you get the money which I send, I trust you will be somewhat comfortable till I come. I will inform you that I am nearly recovered from the most severe sickness that I have experienced for thirty years past. I do not walk out much yet, but am gaining very fast, I am now but a skeleton as to flesh. After Elder Hyde left the office, Brother Richards, my assistant, being sick, or absent very much, I was closely confined to the office, and early in June felt the beginning of poor health which increased upon me until the first of July. But still, as I had no time to spare for being sick, I kept fast to my office, my better judgment teaching me all the while to desist and recruit my health. However, the 7th of July, after having had two or three chills, I concluded that I must yield. Accordingly I selected a healthy residence of one of the Saints, a Brother Ennion, a short distance from Liverpool. I told them I wanted the privilege of being sick at their house, instead of my own in Liverpool, which they readily granted. I immediately laid down, and with constipation of my bowels, and occasional chills, was soon too weak to even turn myself in bed. Some thought that I must die, but I told them not to fear, for I should not die then. In the beginning I told Brother R. to notify many Saints abroad that I was very sick; this I did lest I should be snatched away before their prayers could take effect in my behalf. After that notice I had no further concern, although I went nigh to the gates of death. I took no medicine worth naming. I think that I shall not lose my hair, although I may turn grey. After a few days spent in the country, I hope to take the field again as strong as ever. Indeed I have contributed something to every *Star* yet, and generally given counsel except in my worst sickness. 1 was confined to the house about three weeks. Now I bless the God of heaven as my Savior and restorer. I have great solicitude for you during the sickly season, take good care before being sick; trust in God and if you are taken quite sick, let the Saints around you, and in the public congregations know it speedily.

"Aug. 15th.—I am still gaining health, although I have not been into the country yet owing to bad weather.

"Yesterday's steamer brought the cheering, heart-gladdening letter from Ellen and Aurelia. Be assured that I rejoiced and thanked God, but I felt sad to think you were so scanted for the comforts of life. I suppose you must have written other letters that contain many particulars of interest which I have not received, by what Aurelia wrote. I hope Brother Bullock will not be discouraged, for better days are coming. Your not receiving any more than a sovereign from Elder —— must have been a great disappointment to you, as it was to me. I think the other brethren will not fail in paying the money sent by them. I am afraid there will be no opportunity to send any more till next spring.   *   *   *

"ORSON SPENCER."

LETTER III.

"LIVERPOOL, SEPT. 29th, 1847.

"MY DEARLY BELOVED CHILDREN: On my return from Scotland last night I was happy to find a letter from my dear daughters Ellen and Aurelia. But I was most deeply affected when I heard that Genette and Isabell Bullock were dead. Dear precious children, have I seen them for the last time this side of the grave? They have gone to rest in the Kingdom of God, with my beloved Catherine and her two children. She will know them when they enter heaven and love them and look after their happiness. Tell my dear James and Mary that I deeply mourn with them for their serious loss. I hope that they will not be discouraged nor murmur at the dealings of God, or rather what He suffers to take place. Though He slay us we should trust in Him, and all will be right. Most gladly would I sit down with them in their cabin and try to comfort them. I know what it is to be separated from wife and children by death. But I feel that God is good, though you, my children, have lost the best of mothers and I have lost the best wife ever given to man. I want you, my children, to strive to live by pleasing God, and keeping His commandments. Do not be discouraged at what you have to suffer, but be stout hearted and trust in God, and you will live and reign in life eternal. You say that Brother Bullock works hard and does all he can for you, and that you and Brother Bullock's family live on terms of peace. This comforts me very much, and I hope you will do all you can for them. I know it is a great charge that he has upon him, but the faithful man shall not lose his reward. I have perfect confidence that James will manage all your affairs well, and counsel you in the best manner. My health is pretty good and my labors are very great. After my sickness I began to preach before I could walk many rods, and in one or two instances I have preached while sitting down through weakness; but my strength, through the goodness of God, has increased all the time, and for the last four or five weeks I have preached from two to five times a week, and sat up often as late as two or three o'clock at night in conversation with Saints.

"Wherever I go, the Saints gather around me as though they would worship me. They often walk ten or twenty miles to see me and hear me preach. In the meantime, I write on an average about five or six pages, one-third of the *Star* as original matter lately, and select and arrange other matter for the *Star*, besides answering numerous letters of correspondence daily. Therefore you may judge if I am very busy. I get some presents very frequently, for my children, which I shall bring or send in due time. One sister gave me a shawl in Edinburgh and a very pretty dress pattern for Lucy. Another sister in Glasgow gave me a handsome dress pattern for Ellen. A brother in Manchester has promised me a dress for each of the children, and for Sister Bullock, as soon as I can have a chance to send them. Another man in Scotland says he shall send a fancy dress to some of you. Be good children and the Lord will raise up friends for you. I want very much to see you all, but don't know yet whether they will counsel me to come home next spring or not. Business is very bad in this country universally. Many of the Saints will probably have to go to the poor-house for want of employment. They are very anxious to emigrate to America; and I hope they will have the privilege soon. But the gospel is spreading wonderfully, probably not less than five thousand will be added to the Church this year. I enjoy the work of preaching and writing very much; that which grieves me most is the suffering of my children in the wilderness, and the Saints in America. I hope that President Young has found a location for a Stake of Zion where we may soon go and dwell in peace. For this I labor and pray daily. Brother Andrew Cahoon went with me to Scotland, this climate does not suit his health very well; he now presides over Clitheroe Conference; he is very industrious and faithful.   *   *   *   I have got three new hymn books handsomely bound, with the name of each of my three oldest girls on the outside in gold letters, and gilt edges, etc. I will endeavor to find some good books for Ellen, and also a pretty primer for Lucy. I am glad that Lucy is such a good girl and learns so well. I want Catharine to learn to write, and Howard is probably old enough to write a little. I am very sorry that Aurelia has sick spells and I hope that she will take good care of herself. I thank her for attending to George so faithfully and he must be a good boy and love Aurelia and Ellen for their kindness. I am glad that Howard is also a good boy and don't quarrel with other boys. I want him to harken to Brother Bullock, and be kind to Alexander.* Tell Alexander I mean to bring him something when I come, which will be next spring if the council permit, in time to go with you to the mountains.

---

*Alexander was Brother Bullock's son.

I feel very thankful that you have such good neighbors and friends. May God bless them for their kindness to my motherless children. But I must bring my letter to a close for want of time to say more.

"Your ever affectionate and loving father,

"Orson Spencer."

As can be seen by the above, my father anticipated returning to Winter Quarters, in time to go with us over the mountains; but later on he received a letter from President Young requesting him to stay another year. Therefore in the spring of 1848, we were preparing for our journey across the plains without him. Brother Andrew Cahoon had returned from his mission to Scotland, and by him father had sent money and clothing to fit us out for the journey.

He also sent the following letter:

LETTER IV.

Liverpool, March 25th, 1848.

"My Dear Children: Having a few leisure moments, (which is a rare thing for me,) it gives me very great pleasure to write to you, whom I love with the most inexpressible fondness. You are my dearest treasures upon the earth. Your mother was one of the loveliest of her sex; generous and open hearted in love to all our race. Under all circumstances I always found a welcome asylum in her breast, and she characterized her whole life by those admirable virtues, which secured the spontaneous delight and good will of all who knew her. In you, my dear children, I see many traits of her lovely spirit, and also her features. From her, my own mind has received many a beautifying grace and virtue: and few could live with her as long as I did without being enriched and ennobled by such association. Thus far, your lives are full of promise, your minds are all intelligent and your hearts innocent and pure. The spirit of God can dwell with you, and assist you to emulate celestial worthies. I desire so to live that my example and teaching shall tend to give you a mould and polish which will make heaven happier at your approach, and angels to rejoice over you as in the acquisition of the richest of pearls. Dear children, for my own sake then, don't be discouraged or impatient, but try to live through your appointed days, for your lot is cast in an age of sorrow mingled indeed with the sweet solace of redeeming triumphs. Deprived of your mother by death, and your father by obedience to the counsels of the church, your pathway is perilous and stormy.

"Sometimes without shoes to your feet and sometimes without bread, surrounded with savage foes, without any assurance that I will be restored to you for a long time yet to come, you may indeed often wonder why your lot is thus; and why want and orphanage and peril and a homeless pilgrimage should all come upon you at once, and that, while you are at an age so tender.

"While I am writing, I suppose you are struggling with all the energy and diligence your tender minds are capable of to escape to the mountains; being required to leave the little cabin and garden and field, that I hoped would shield you till I could come to comfort you. But you must recross the river and build anew, or flee to the mountains, the latter I prefer, as the country is sickly and the times perilous. Still your means are very scanty for such a journey to a land where you must make the only home you will have, without me to counsel or accompany you. If you go over the mountains I may not hear from you or you from me for nearly a year and a half. My dear children, I trust that God, who counsels us to walk the narrow way, will be your shield and defence, and provide for your wants and keep you all alive till we meet again, where the fury of the oppressor cannot overtake us, and the storms of heavenly indignation may pass us by in the day of great distress. If I am counseled to endure this long separation and to expose you to such privations, my prayer shall be the more fervent in your behalf, and with strength of heart and soul, I shall plead for your lives to be spared, and your minds kept unpolluted. Love one another and bear each other's faults. Cherish the spirit of God by patience and kindness. Never yield to sin or do anything that you would be ashamed to ask God about or tell me of. Let no one entice you to do wrong, whoever it may be. Keep together, live together and do not separate. Be friends to one another, and caution the younger sisters and brothers against accidents, against bad conduct and bad company. Believe that God can hear and help you when you need it, and tell you many things which are necessary for you to know and do. Learn to trust in God for all good things, and to be thankful for all favors. And if God should not allow me to return any more on the earth, you will be visited from heaven when it is requisite. Be cheerful and happy and cherish virtue and truth and strive to be an ornament to my family forever. Contract no alliance incompatible with the interest of the family. And if you maintain a blameless life you will survive all discouragements, and those that bless you shall be blesesd, and they that harm you shall be cursed, and God and angels will be your friends and your parents shall never slumber over your condition, worlds without end.

"Your journey will be long and tedious, you will need to be very careful not to get lost from your camp on the journey; and also be cautious in regard to the hostile Indians, serpents or dangerous roots and herbs. Do not walk out at night away from the camp while on the journey. You will scarcely be saved with the utmost faith, diligence and economy. My anxieties about you from the time you leave till I see you will be unceasingly great.

"My oldest daughters; on you is rolled a great responsibility, seemingly beyond your years. Be womanly, kind and patient, act the part of mother to the younger children. Teach them good principles and instruct them how to act. Avoid in yourselves the weakness and folly of youth as much as possible. Never forget or slight my counsel, for this is the commandment of God. I think I write to you according to the mind of God. I am not permitted to speak face to face, but I write unto you as a father with soberness and godly fear. Treasure up my sayings and teach them to the younger children and read this letter to them, at least, three or four times a year till I come to you. Teach George to stand by Howard as his counselor and right hand man. George shall be distinguished for shrewdness and quick discernment and a great help to Howard and to you all. Watch over Lucy, for she is the choicest emblem of peace, and you shall have the honor of bringing her up to womanhood. Howard and George:—be good boys, yea, more than this, be manly and very kind to your sisters. They have taken care of you as a mother should do, they have counseled you, provided for your wants and taken charge of you in sickness and in health, and you ought to love them and strive to please them in all things. Be obedient to them in my absence till you are grown up, then honor and protect them till the day of your death. Counsel with them in all difficult matters, and never lift your hand against them in anger or strife, and know that your prosperity lies in your union. Strive to get knowledge. Study well when you have an opportunity.

"Spread your feelings freely before one another and let your most secret plans and designs be entrusted to each other, but keep them to yourselves and divulge them not abroad. And whatever you all unite in, will almost invariably be right. Let the boys not waste their strength in wrestling or scuffling, although a little of these exercises are good, but godliness will profit them more. Go and hear preaching when you can, and talk about what you hear. If you go over the mountains before I do, you will use your best judgment in selecting a lot. Adhere to Brother Bullock and his wife, for I want them to go with you wherever you go, or stay and never desert you. You will not have means probably to assist anybody but Brother Bullock, with what I send you in money and clothes. Don't listen to any false tales against Brother Bullock. He is good and faithful.

"I should like to have the girls and also Howard pay particular attention to arithmetic. This is more important than geography or grammar.

"You will need good oil cloth covers to your wagons, and a good tent I think. Have as many cows as your means will permit; but if you should not go over the mountains this spring, you will still need all the means you can get.

"The prospect is very good for a great ingathering of converts in England, during the coming season; but business just now is worse than ever. Revolutions are going forward in Europe, and Monarchs are trembling on their thrones. The people almost universally demand a change of government and of rulers. The agitation is so very great that business is kept very much in suspense. Almost every paper brings news of the overthrow of some kingdom and the flight of some king. Commerce and trade are consequently at a stand. The people are looking for general war.

"My health at present is only tolerably good. I am very thin in flesh in consequence of many labors and cares. Since I have been here, I have spared no pains whatever to keep the work of God rolling forth with success and power; and prosperity has attended my labors thus far beyond my utmost anticipations. I have had no time for play or rest, but think when Elder Orson Pratt comes that I shall have a little respite. Your last letter was three months and a half coming. Send your letters by mail in the quickest conveyance. If you don't go over the mountains, write once a month without fail. You will have enough to write about; tell me about all little matters. Write the last thing, and tell me particularly all about your outfit. It will be my constant desire to live in order to do you good, and provide for your wants. I want you all to be very good children. I am very anxious to see you once more, but I will not disobey my lawful counselors. George is now eight years old; if he has not been baptized yet I want to have him baptized soon. Do the boys learn well at school?

"The Boston steamer has not arrived, consequently I must send this letter without hearing anything from you. In haste. God bless you my children. Farewell!

"Your Ever Affectionate Father,

"ORSON SPENCER."

CHAPTER VIII.

JOURNEY ACROSS THE PLAINS.

We left Winter Quarters about the first of May, 1848, traveling in President Young's company. He had made the trip across the plains the year before, as the leader of the Pioneers, and had returned for the rest of his family, and to see after the poor Saints who could not help themselves.

On this journey I met and became acquainted with Thomas Rogers, who afterwards became my husband. He drove a team for Andrew Cahoon, who was captain of our ten; the company was divided into tens and fifties.

There were many ups and downs in our travels; when the weather was pleasant we enjoyed ourselves very much, although having to walk over the roughest part of the road, as the wagons were heavily loaded. In camping at night, the wagons of the company were formed in a circle, with the tongues inside. The cattle (for our teams consisted mostly of oxen and cows,) were either herded or tied, to prevent any surprise by the Indians, who were often seen prowling around, watching their chance to stampede our animals. During the journey the company would stop once in awhile for a few days to recruit their teams and give the women a chance to wash, iron, bake, etc.

On one of these occasions, we camped on Looking-glass Creek, which emptied into the Platt River about a mile below. The people had been counseled not to go far from camp; but either forgetting or not heeding the counsel, about a dozen girls, myself included, took it into our heads, one bright moonlight night, to go to the mouth of the creek and bathe in the river, thinking the distance would make us safe from interruption. The Platt River was very wide in places and the water quite shallow, being interspersed with sand-bars. The company forded it many times in the course of their travels.

One elderly lady, namely Sister Mima Young, generally called Aunt Mima, went with us as a protector, or to stand guard while we should take our bath. A nice place was selected and we were soon splashing around in the water as happy as could be. Presently one of the girls said, "Let us play baptize." Some of the rest consented and were soon ducked under the water although I don't remember that any ceremony was used. We were soon interrupted in our sport, however, by some one exclaiming, "See! what is that? what is that coming?" All looked in the direction pointed out, and sure enough something white and strange looking was coming, right towards us across the river, and only a short distance away. Then such a screaming and rushing for the shore, was perhaps never witnessed before nor since, some of the girls almost falling down in the water from fright. I was like one paralyzed, could not speak or move for a few seconds, and was nearly the last one out of the water. But all gained the shore in safety; looking back we saw the object which had so frightened us go up the creek, and disappear.

Our conjectures were varied in regard to what it might have been; some thought it much larger than it seemed to others. But whatever it was it floated towards us until we started for the shore, then turned and went up the creek. All agreed that it was a warning, and felt that we had done wrong in playing baptize. We had also disobeyed counsel by going so far away from camp, and harm might have come to us. We wended our way back to the wagons quite sobered, reflecting and talking these things over as we went along; but the mystery of what we had seen was never solved.

Sometimes in our travels there was much picturesque scenery to enjoy; many grand looking rocks, one in particular was called Chimney Rock; so named on account of its great height, and peculiar shape. There was a number of names written on this rock, by those who preceded us to the Valley, which made us rejoice, for it was like a guide post in the desert.

In the course of nearly a five months' journey we arrived in Salt Lake Valley, having traveled over a thousand miles. It was a happy time as we merged from Emigration Canyon and took a view of the Valley that was to be the future home of the Saints. Then as we neared the

Fort, we passed through large corn-fields which looked inviting and quite home like. The Fort consisted of log rooms joined together until a square was formed, with gateways to enter. We occupied one of these rooms which Uncle Daniel had put up for our use, he having come to the valley the year before. There was no floor in the house we lived in, and only one six lighted window. Our stove was put up in one corner, in this we baked biscuit, and when they were done we would sit around the stove and eat them. Once in awhile Aunt Emily, or Cousin Antoinette would send us some vegetables.

The reader must bear in mind that this was only a desert land the year before, having been condemned by mountaineers, who offered $1000 for the first bushel of corn that could be raised here; and that no one but people inspired of God, would ever have made the attempt to raise anything in these valleys here.

The winter passed very pleasantly; we attended meetings, and occasionally a dancing party, as those parties were indulged in to help pass the time away. Ellen and I also attended writing school two evenings a week, which was taught by Hiram B. Clawson.

I was naturally of an independent disposition, and found ways to get a little money of my own by taking in sewing and making bracelets and necklaces out of hair, some of which I sold for a trifle. The hair work I had learned while in Nauvoo.

A city had been laid out in the valley of the Great Salt Lake, with wide streets and a number of public squares.

A ten acre lot was reserved for the Temple and other public buildings. The people had many trials in the early settling of Utah, losing their crops the first year by drought and crickets. Still they persevered, and by the blessings of God, in a short time towns and villages were interspersed throughout the Territory. The water in the creeks, which at first were but tiny streams, increased until there was plenty for all purposes.

Our city lot was on what is now called main street, and fronting emigration street on the south. We had one small adobe room put up, into which we moved, and thought ourselves quite comfortable.

In the summer of 1849, the welcome news reached us that our father was coming home with a company of emigrants, and would be here by the latter part of September.

* * *

CHAPTER IX.

ORSON SPENCER IN ENGLAND.

I WILL now go back to the time when my father left us in our log cabin at Winter Quarters, and follow him to England.

Previous to his arrival in Liverpool, news had preceded him that "Orson Spencer was dead." This mistake was supposed to have occurred through some one's hearing of the death of my uncle Hyrum Spencer. The news went across the water in a letter written by Brother John Parker, of St. Louis, to Elder Franklin D. Richards, who was at that time presiding over a conference in Glasgow, Scotland.

The letter with an obituary notice was soon after published in the *Star*. On account of the news of my father's death, Brother Franklin D. was called to England to take the presidential chair and attend to the duties of the press. From which duties, however, he was soon relieved, as my father arrived in Liverpool safe and sound on the 23rd of January 1847. For further information, I will copy an address, which was published in the *Millennial Star*, No 3, Vol. 9.

ADDRESS.

"It now becomes our duty and privilege to address a few words to the Saints in the British Isles, through the medium of the *Star*. On account of the supposed decease of our worthy brother, Orson Spencer, we were called from our field of labor in Scotland, to act in our present calling and station, as appointed and published by our beloved president, Orson Hyde, in the last number of the *Star*. But it affords us superlative pleasure to advise our readers, that

Elder Spencer is alive and in our midst enjoying excellent health and buoyant spirits, as is also our beloved brother Elder Andrew Cahoon, who accompanied Brother Spencer from the camps of the Saints to this island. They landed in Liverpool on Saturday evening, the 23rd instant, after a protracted voyage of about forty days, encountering storms and gales; by the kindness of the Father's care, they were preserved from any serious disaster. Few men in the nineteenth century possess that degree of longevity which enables them to read in the public prints their own obituary notice, but it has been Elder Spencer's privilege to read the feelings of his brethren concerning him, when they never expected to see him again in mortality; and we speak with great confidence, when we say, that he enjoys an ardent and a faithful place in the affections of thousands upon these islands, that can say of him, 'Whom not having seen, we love;' and we feel that all faithful Saints will bestow upon him their confidence and most cordial and hearty support and co-operation, giving diligent heed to his counsels in all things. For ourselves we have to say, (and we speak knowingly,) that Elder Spencer's appointment was by the counsel of the quorum of the Twelve Apostles in the land of Zion, to take the presidency of the Church and charge of the publishing department in this country, and we gladly surrender to him the responsibility and honor of that important trust, for we are deeply sensible that where much is given, much is required; and we feel to say, let the rich blessings which President Hyde so freely bestowed upon ourselves in the last number of the *Star* rest in all their richness and fullness upon our beloved Brother Spencer, and may he realize joy and blessing in the performance of those duties which are before him; and have great satisfaction in seeing the work of the Lord prosper under his hands; and it will still be our studious aim to render to the uttermost our mite of influence and exertion, subservient to the cause of our Lord Jesus Christ, under the directions, and according to the dictation of him, and them, who are appointed to preside over the Church, in the kingdom, ever mindful that

'Honor or fame, not from condition rise,
Act well your part, there all the honor lies.'

"We feel to tender to the Saints our thanks and blessings, in the name of the Lord, for the kindness and favors which we have at any time experienced at their hands, especially our brethren in Scotland, among whom our labors have hitherto been for the greater part bestowed, and remain, your brother in Christ, and fellow-servant in the kingdom of God,

"FRANKLIN D. RICHARDS,"
January 27, 1847.

Father had been in England one year when the following was addressed to him:

LETTER FROM PRESIDENT BRIGHAM YOUNG TO ORSON SPENCER.

"WINTER QUARTERS, Jan. 23, 1848.

"DEAR BROTHER:—Yours of the 1st of November, 1847, came to hand on the 11th instant. I was much pleased to hear of the prosperity of the work in the British Islands—of your good health and your desires to labor in the vineyard. Brother Heber and myself called upon your family, read your letter, found them all well and in lively spirits; the house and the children were clean and neat, and they presented a comparatively comfortable aspect.

"The difficulty of getting grinding this winter, in a great measure prevents us from being as comfortable as we otherwise might be, but another grist mill starts tomorrow, which will be the fourth run of the stones in the city. I asked the children how they would like me to send you word to stay another year, as I thought it was best to do so, and take them and Brother Bullock's family over the mountains in the spring. Ellen replied, "If it is thought best, we would like it so, for we want to do for the best," and they all said amen to it. I told Ellen to buy a good milch cow, and I would pay for it, and reminded her of my saying last winter, that if she lacked anything she was to let me know. It is thought advisable for you to stay another year, and I will take your family on in the spring. We anticipate sending

Brother Orson Pratt and several other Elders to England, who will leave here when we leave for the mountains, and of sending Brother Woodruff to Nova Scotia, Canadas, etc., at the same time. Brother George A. Smith is having some log cabins built on the other side of the river, and intends in a few days to remove over there, and stay for a year or two amongst the brethren, as those who do not go onward must vacate this place and go over to the Pottowatomie purchase.

"Orson Hyde will stay there also, and with Brother George will take care of the branches and push the Saints onward.

"In December last we appointed a day to hold a conference on the other side of the river, in a large double block house, occupied by one of the brethren, where the Saints congregated in such large numbers that we found it impracticable to continue our conference, the house being so crowded and many shouting at the windows to get in, so we adjourned for three weeks to build a house capable of holding the Saints. Accordingly, on the 24th, we convened again at the "Log Tabernacle," which they erected in a short time, during the severest weather we have had this winter. It is a well-constructed, capacious log house, sixty by forty feet inside and will seat one thousand persons, with a recess or stand twenty by ten feet for the priesthood and a clerk's bench; it is certainly an ornament to this new country, and shows a little of Mormonism. I told them at the conference that the brethren had built, fenced and made as many improvements in the short time they had been here (about a year) as they would in Missouri in about ten years; and it is a fact; and they have raised a crop equal to any we raised in Illinois.

At this conference we suggested to the brethren the propriety of organizing the Church with a First Presidency and a Patriarch, as hinted at in our general epistle; and the expediency of such a move at this time was so clearly seen by the brethren that they hailed it as an action which the state of the work at present demanded, and as a means to liberate the hands of the quorum of the Twelve, who now feel at liberty to go abroad and herald the truth to the ends of the earth, and build up the kingdom in all the world. Accordingly, Brigham Young was nominated to be the First President of the Church, and he nominated Heber C. Kimball and Willard Richards to be his two counselors, which nominations were seconded and carried without a dissentient voice.

"Father John Smith as then nominated to be Patriarch of the whole Church—in the same capacity as **Father Joseph Smith** was, also Brother Hyrum—seconded and carried unanimously. The Spirit of the Lord at this time rested upon the congregation in a powerful manner, insomuch that the Saints' hearts were filled with joy unspeakable; every power of their mind and nerve of their body was awakened and absorbed; a dead stillness reigned in the congregation while the President spoke. He said: 'This is one of the happiest days of my life; it is according as Heber prophesied yesterday, our teachings today have been good. I never heard better. Is not the bliss of heaven and the breezes of Zion wafted here? Who feels hatred, malice or evil? If you come to the door with a bad spirit, it would not come in with you; no, it could not mingle here; but when you enter, your feelings become as calm and gentle as the zephyrs of paradise; and I feel glory, hallelujah! Nothing more has been done today than what I knew would be done when Joseph died.

"'We have been driven from Nauvoo here, but the hand of the Lord is in it,—visible as the sun shining this morning; it is visible to my natural eyes; it's all right; and I expect when we see the result of all we pass through in this probationary state, we will discover the hand of the Lord in it all, and shout Amen, it's all right! We shall make the upper courts ring; we have something to do before then. I don't calculate to go beyond the bounds of time and space where we will have no opposition,—no devils to contend with; and I have no fault to find with the providences of the Lord, nor much fault to find with the people; and if the devils will keep out of my path I will not quarrel with them. As the Lord's will is my will all the time, as He dictates so I will perform. If He don't guide the ship, we'll go down in the whirlpool. Joseph told the Twelve, the year before he died, 'There is not one key or power to be bestowed on this Church to lead the people into the celestial gate, but I have given you, showed you, and talked it over to you; the kingdom is set up, and you have the perfect pattern, and you can go and build up the kingdom and go in at the celestial gate, taking your train with you.'

"The instrumental band was then called upon to perform, when its heavenly vibrations fell upon the tender nerve of the ear, accompanied by the Spirit of God, and the Saints shouted, 'Hosanna, Hosanna, Hosanna to God and the Lamb, Amen, Amen, and Amen!' led by George A. Smith. The conference lasted four days. We had indeed an excellent time; and on the 16th of January attended another meeting, convened by the Seventies, which they called a Jubilee, but I told them it could not be considered a Jubilee spoken of in Revelations, for all bands were not broken, and I called it Jubilo,—when the Saints assembled and spent the Sabbath in preaching and exhortation; and on Monday, Tuesday, Wednesday and Thursday, had preaching and teaching concerning the organization of companies for traveling westward,—music and other recreations. We had a blessed meeting—all hearts were comforted and lifted up above our trials and persecutions, and we went home rejoicing in the benefits and privileges of the liberty of the Gospel of Jesus Christ; and I pray they may thereby be stimulated to pursue the path of righteousness, and fill up the remainder of their days in promoting the kingdom of peace and happiness on the earth.

"We learn from Mr. Glenday, who has been to Oregon City, Willamette Valley, this year, from Missouri, and who came into camp on the 14th current, that he saw some of our brethren at Fort Call on the 15th of November last, that had been there buying meat and flour. He also saw three brethren working at Fort Bridger, (115 miles from the valley,) at which place he learned that the Mormons, in the valley, had got between 200 and 300 acres of fall wheat sown, and that there was a company going to San

Francisco Bay for seed wheat to sow in the spring, and there was plenty of provisions in the valley.

"The brethren in this region of country have been much more healthy this summer and fall than ever in Nauvoo, and this has been a great blessing, as you know disease and sickness have been a heavy tax on the Saints. The weather this winter has been very mild indeed; these two weeks past have been like the opening spring, which favors us greatly, especially those who have to leave their farms and improvements here, recross the Missouri, and begin anew on the Pottowatamie lands.

"The brethren are busy fixing up their wagons and making preparations for their journey, and having a plenty of corn and fodder, their teams are doing well.

"The Omahas have been peaceable this winter, and have not killed any cattle, and our circumstances, in comparison with last winter, are very prosperous and good.

"Your Brother in the Lord,
"BRIGHAM YOUNG."

LETTER FROM WILFORD WOODRUFF.

Winter Quarters, Omaha Nation,
April 24, 1848.

"Dear Brother Orson Spencer:—While impressed with a deep sense of duty I owe you as a brother, a friend and fellow workman in the great cause of God, I seat myself to acknowledge the reception of your kind letter to me, under date of January 18, 1848; and while I view letter writing as one of the choicest blessings of God to man, I feel thankful that I can exchange thoughts and words with my dear friends from whom I am separated by seas, tide and distance, yet it is almost painful to reflect that while I have a desire to converse freely with Brother Spencer, Brother Jones, and thousands of good Saints that surround you, and unbosom my feelings unto you upon a variety of subjects, that I am confined, as it were to the narrow limits of a sheet of paper. But as I cannot at present speak face to face with you I will content myself, as well as I can, by saying a few words with my pen. Men of God, who possess the spirit and power of the Holy

Ghost, can form a good idea what element they are moving in—what spirits surround them; and they have only to behold a man's face, feel of his spirit, read the productions of his pen, in order to know what port his ship is bound for. And I can say of a truth, with every feeling and sentiment of my heart, that whenever I have read, or heard read, any of the letters or productions of Brother Spencer's pen either addressed to myself, President Young, or any of the Twelve, or his own family, or published in the *Star*, I feel perfectly satisfied that they were dictated by the spirit and power of God, and spoke in language, not to be misunderstood, that all was right at head quarters in Liverpool, and that the Lord was guiding Brother Spencer; and the same spirit was manifest in the writings of our worthy Brother Dan Jones, of Wales, and the Brothers Richards, and I may say the Elders in general throughout your field of labors. You may rest assured that these things have caused much joy in our hearts, and when I express my feelings upon this subject I believe I speak the sentiments of all the

Presidency in this land. Yes, Brother Spencer, we know the Lord is with you, and with your fellow-laborers in that land, and you have done a great and glorious work, and brought much good to pass; and for all these things you will have your reward. We have felt a deep interest in your field of labor, and the labor and field of Captain Dan Jones. I rejoice much in the progress he has made in Wales, and in the fruit of the labors of the faithful Elders throughout the British dominions. And I feel to say, Brother Spencer, Brother Jones, and all the faithful laborers in the vineyard with you, be not weary in well-doing, for if you continue faithful in your tribulations and sacrifices, the day will come, and perhaps it may not be far distant, when you will rejoice before God and all the holy ones. Because of the missions you are now filling, the labors you are performing among the nations of the earth you will be satisfied with the goodness of the Lord, and your reward in the hour of the holy resurrection. And when the Lord cometh, bringing his reward with him, yea, it will be a source of consolation to you through all eternity to know that you have been a messenger of salvation to many, that your garments are clear of the blood of the generation in which you live; that you have stood with your garments unspotted; that your tabernacle has not been defiled; that no man has taken your crown; that you have kept the celestial law; and, in fine, that you have filled the measure of your creation. You will have the blessings of the Lord with you, and the prayers of the Saints in your behalf. I have watched with deep interest the progress of the work throughout England, Scotland and Wales. President Young received your letter under date of March. We also received an account of the French revolution, and the signs of the times throughout Europe, which was read with interest.

"As concerning matters with us, I will begin with the time we last parted in Winter Quarters. You know my situation then. But I was greatly blessed of the Lord, for in twenty days from the time I received my serious injury I again commenced work of the hardest kind in building and preparing for winter. I continued to labor hard with my hands until the departure of the pioneers' camp, in the following spring, without feeling any serious effects from my hurt. I performed my journey with the tents and camp of the pioneers over two thousand miles, making the road entirely new over five hundred miles, and performed much hard labor in the valley; and this was accomplished in less than seven months' time. And it was clearly visible to every discerning mind that the Lord was with us, for though many of the pioneers were sick when we left Winter Quarters, yet with all our sickness and exposures of such a journey, buffalo stampedes, grizzly bear frights, Indian attacks, not a soul was lost, but all returned safe to our homes; and, what was more remarkable still, we used ox, mule and horse teams through the whole journey, and not a hoof was lost of any beast belonging to the pioneer camp of Israel, except in two or three instances horses were shot accidentally, or killed, by not hearkening to counsel. But an account of our journey, and a description of the valley, have already been sent you, and I need not repeat it here. The Spirit and power of God was with us on that journey, was with us in that valley, and has been with us since we returned home. We also found on our return that the Lord had blessed the Saints at Winter Quarters and the region round about, in our absence. The earth had brought forth in its strength, and the laborer had been well rewarded. Winter Quarters on our return presented one of the most novel scenes I ever beheld. While standing upon the ridge west of the city it appeared almost a dense mass of corn stalks, hay stacks, covered wagons and log cabins, and apparently a spark of fire in the combustibles would soon present to the eye, as did Moscow, a sea of fire. But notwithstanding our exposure, we have thus far been delivered from the ravages of that element. Three messengers arrived a few days since from the City of the Great Salt Lake. They left the middle of January, came through the mountains in the dead of winter. They brought many letters with them, all bringing the most cheering news of matters in that place.

Population 3,000; sickness and death seldom known. Letters stated one death during the winter. The coldest day known, the 1st of November; very little snow. Winter supposed to have broke early in January. Valley green with grass four inches high 15th of January. Horses, mules, oxen, sheep, and all stock wintered well in the open valley. One flouring mill and three saw mills in operation; and plenty of the best quality of lime, and clay for the best quality of brick, tile, and for earthen crockery and queensware; good slate quarries and grindstones; salt and saltpetre. The brethren had built near 1,000 dwellings, had sown about 1,500 acres of wheat, expected to put in as much more, and 3,000 or 4,000 acres of corn. Wheat looked well. No disturbance from the natives that surrounded them. We are now looking for other arrivals from there daily, who will start the last of February or 1st of March. It is a general time of health through the camps of Israel in Winter Quarters; but few deaths through the winter. The first camp or company who go west this spring expect to start in a few days in company with Presidents Brigham Young, Heber C. Kimball, Willard Richards, and others of the Apostles. Winter Quarters will be evacuated; all who remain settle in Pottowatamie County, Iowa. Orson Hyde and George A. Smith will preside there; Orson Pratt in England; Wilford Woodruff the Eastern States, Canada, Nova Scotia, New Brunswick and adjacent islands. We are expecting a boat daily, upon which Orson Pratt is calculating to take passage for St. Louis, and continue his journey to Liverpool with as little delay as possible. I expect to start for Boston as soon as the first company leaves, and trust I shall be able to correspond with my friends in England from that point. We had quite an interesting conference on the 6th inst., at the log tabernacle.

"There are many things I would like to speak of that my limits will not allow at this time; however, I should do injustice to my own feelings, and neglect a duty towards you, should I close without touching upon one subject that deeply interests you, that is your family. A remark in your letter to me, and more especially those made in the address to President Young concerning your children, planted in my mind a determination to visit them. Accordingly, last evening Mrs. Woodruff and myself walked down to your house; and, to my surprise, instead of finding Sister Spencer (with whom we had spent many precious moments in holy places) at the head of her family, I found she was sleeping in the dust, and your eldest daughter, who was only thirteen years of age when you left, stood in the place of a mother and counselor to her five younger brothers and sisters. I enquired into all their circumstances and difficulties since you left, which they had been called to pass through; and while they related past events to me, and read their file of letters from their father, I was filled with sensations better imagined than described.

"When I considered what they had passed through, their young and tender ages, the share they had taken in the sufferings of the Saints, I regarded them not only a company of young pilgrims, but a company of young martyrs; and although in childhood, their faith, patience, forbearance and long-suffering and wisdom in the midst of all their trials, was such as would have done honor to a Saint of thirty years in the strength and power of his days, or been a crown of glory upon the grey hairs of him of riper years. A parent may well consider such a family of children a blessing from God. I believe they have honored you in your absence. Ellen said she had received a letter within a few days from you, and had answered it.

"Your children were all well yesterday. I enquired into their present circumstances. They said they had plenty of meal but no flour. I told them to come to my house and I would divide with them. The eldest son came down today, and I gave him some flour and pork. I would have been glad to have divided with them a long time before had I but known their circumstances. You may think it strange why I have not known; but our affairs for the last year or two have been like the rolling billows, and each sea has brought as much weight upon every faithful man's back as he was able to carry, unless he by chance might meet with a calm for a moment, and give him a chance to look around to see if any man had a heavier load than himself, and if so, to stretch out his hand and help to carry it. Ellen told me she expected the family would go on with the first company this season to the mountains.

"I must close. Mrs. Woodruff, with myself, sends respects, love and blessings to Brother and Sister Spencer, and wish to be remembered to Brother and Sister Enion, Brother and Sister Hall, and all who enquire after us.

"Yours in the bonds of the Priesthood,
"WILFORD WOODRUFF."

CHAPTER X.

EXTRACTS FROM ARTICLES AND LETTERS.

FROM AN ARTICLE WRITTEN FOR THE STAR, BY THOMAS D. BROWN.

"SHREWSBURY, JUNE 1st, 1848.
* * * "On the Good Friday afternoon about 4 o'clock, nearly one hundred Saints assembled from Poolquay, Ellesmere, and other branches in North Wales, belonging to the Liverpool Conference, and sat down to a comfortable tea. Elder Thomas, who presided over the Shrewsbury Branch, called upon Elder T. D. Brown to preside, who addressed the Saints on the great and good work of the Lord in which they were engaged, and congratulated them on the auspicious events of that day—their assembling to open a large room to preach in, and to a branch of the Church now numbering twenty-four, who, but a few short months ago were in darkness. * * * * *

"Elder Thomas then followed, and gave a short history of the work in that region. * *

"Elder Orson Spencer, the President of the Church in Europe, then addressed the Saints. He was a stranger to them in person, and though many of them were intimate with his writings, they now, hearing his voice for the first time, seemed to hang upon his lips ; and as the glorious principles of salvation were developed, for upwards of two hours a breathless silence pervaded the meeting, and the Spirit of God like a fire was burning ; yea, truly, all felt, and many exclaimed, 'It is good to be here,' and one sister said, 'Arduous as has been our journey, I would travel fifty miles again to share the intelligence and joys in such another meeting'. * * * * *

"Elder Caleb Parry, next addressed the meeting and sang a song of Zion ; and we remembered that though he was in a strange land he had not hung his harp upon a willow. We had heard that he cheered the Saints in these regions by his melodies and by the truths of God. * *

"At nine o'clock we separated, rejoicing in the

hope that we should meet again in the heights of Zion, and rejoice even more than we had this day done as the sons and daughters of God.

"Elder Spencer retired to the country to recruit and invigorate his health, and a constitution not strong at best, but at present much drawn upon by the arduous duties of the presidency in these lands. We feel to say, God bless and strengthen him, and let all the faithful say amen."

Apostle Orson Pratt had been appointed by the First Presidency of the Church to preside over the British mission. My father speaks of his safe arrival, in the editorial of the *Star*, Aug. 1st, 1848.

The first General Epistle of President Orson Pratt (after his arrival) to the Saints in Great Britain:

* * * "The Saints in this land have been highly favored and extensively benefited by the indefatigable and praiseworthy labors of our much esteemed and dearly beloved brother, Elder Orson Spencer, whose wise and judicious course in his presidential administration over the

Saints in this land will ever live in remembrance of all the faithful. His integrity and sterling virtues have erected for him an enduring monument that can never perish. The eloquent and powerful reasonings displayed in all his writings, the bold, energetic and beautiful style diffused through every part, and the meek and humble spirit which seems to pervade almost every sentence, clearly indicate a sound mind, enlightened by the Spirit of Truth, and filled with wisdom by the inspiration of the Almighty. The inestimable truths which he has so ably developed in his writings, will prove an invaluable treasure to thousands, and live in the memory of all future generations. We are happy to inform the Saints that Brother Spencer will, if his health permits, tarry in this land yet a few months, and we hope to see many articles from his pen upon various subjects, feeling assured that they will be hailed with delight by the anxious multitudes, many of whom have already tasted the soul cheering knowledge he has formerly communicated, which has served to greatly sharpen their appetites for more."

"LIVERPOOL, Sunday, 10th Sept., 1848.

"BELOVED PRESIDENT ORSON PRATT :—I have this day spent an hour at the bedside of our afflicted brother, Orson Spencer, and at this moment feel moved to suggest, if you approve, that the British Saints testify by their works as they do by their faithful prayers, that they love him indeed and of a truth, for his labor and works for the kingdom of God among them. I am sure I express but faintly the feelings of my brethren and sisters in these lands when I say we do love him, and feel so grateful to him that we wish him to carry to the heights of Zion some lasting token of our affection, to cheer his own soul, and in a measure to reward his young and numerous family for their valor in permitting him so long to absent himself from them, and that, too, so soon after the death of their loving mother.

"If one penny from each of the 17,000 Saints in these lands would scarcely be felt, even by the poorest, how much good would this do to Elder Spencer and his family? And if this would do so much good, surely sixpence from those who felt so and could spare it, would do more.

"As there are but three months to do this small but good work, I leave the *modus operandi* with you to suggest to the conferences.

"THOMAS D. BROWN."

"The suggestions in the foregoing letter meet my approbation, and if they meet the approbation of the conferences, they can appoint their agents to receive collections for our beloved Brother Spencer. These agents can forward the amounts by post-office orders or otherwise as they shall please. In blessing Brother Spencer they shall be blessed.—ED."

A PRAYER.

In behalf of Brother Orson Spencer.

"RAMSEY, ISLE OF MAN, Oct. 9, 1848.

"DEAR BROTHER PRATT:—I send the following prayer for insertion in the *Star*, if it meets your approbation; and I assure you whatever be its merits or demerits as a metrical composition, that it breathes the real and sincere sentiments of my heart, and of thousands more. Will you have the kindness to give my love to Brother Spencer. (Years before I saw him I loved him on account of his great advocacy of the truth; and I feel that he possesses the Spirit of God, and a highly intelligent mind.)

"By so doing you will oblige yours in the renewed covenant,

"W. G. MILLS."

Eternal Father, by whose skill
  Our mortal frames from dust were made;
Who speak'st and at thy sovereign will
  We in the dust again are laid!

And on the earth at thy command
  We have our being, live and move.
Who dare arrest thy mighty hand
  That rules among the hosts above?

We own thy power, with humble hearts,
  And bow submissive at thy throne;
Yet claim the gift thy grace imparts;
  We can approach thee through thy Son.

In Jesus' name our prayers ascend
  To thee, who do'st our sorrows know;
For Brother Spencer's health contend—
  Beloved by Saints and angels too.

A noble champion in thy cause,
   Preserve him for the sons of men;
A lover of thy holy laws,
   Restore him to our midst again.

Send down thy Spirit's cleansing aid
   To guide the motions of his heart;
Let it his system now pervade,
   To heal in each diseased part.

Oh! seal on his devoted head
   The gift of health, we do implore;
And raise him from his weary bed,
   To tread again his native shore.

Far as the east is from the west
   Bid the afflicting power to move;
Oh! let our fervent, pure request
   In his behalf effectual prove.

As when of old the prophet prayed,
   The vapoury clouds withheld their rain;
So when he sought thy promised aid
   They pour'd their cheering draughts again.

As when the sick and feeble felt
   Thy Son His healing Spirit pour;
So we believe that, if thou wilt,
   Thou canst our brother now restore.

Thy promises are, gracious Lord,
  "Whate'er ye ask, I will supply."
And we believe the unerring word—
  Thou art a God that canst not lie.

We leave him in thy care, with faith,
  That thou wilt heal his suff'ring frame;
Preserve him yet awhile from death,
  We humbly ask in Jesus' name.

Subsequently my father's health having improved, preparations were made for his return to his native land, with a company of English Saints, and on the 1st of January, 1849, his farewell address was published, a part of which I will copy:

FAREWELL ADDRESS BY ORSON SPENCER, LATE PRESIDENT OF THE EUROPEAN CHURCHES.

"BELOVED SAINTS:—The time is at hand when, by the permission of the First Presidency in Zion, I shall be fully discharged from the duties of my mission to the British nation. I shall return to the bosom of my family, and to the Priesthood in Zion, after an absence of nearly three years. I go to the place of gathering for all nations, pointed out by nearly all the prophets which have spoken since the world began. I go to the Saints' hiding place, there to contemplate from the heights of the mountains of Israel the glory of that kingdom which is the Lord's with the saviors thereof; and also the consummation that is decreed upon the whole earth. There shall be a priesthood of saviors stand up in holy places and judge the nations of the earth. From thence shall the word of the Lord go forth, and the kingdom shall be given to the people of the Saints of the Most High God. Lively sensations thrill through my bosom, in view of the day when I shall greet the nobles of Israel in the heights of the earth, and once more press my little ones to the paternal breast. * * * The language of the General Epistle of the Twelve requires the Saints throughout the British dominions to make all diligence to effect a prompt and speedy emigration to Zion. Great fixedness of purpose and contempt of difficulties must nerve up your efforts, or many will never reach the city of refuge. But let not the poor be discouraged who are laboring with their might to build up the kingdom. The Lord knows their works, their patience and their sufferings, and their salvation is continually in remembrance before Him. Your deliverance from this land, where perils hang in portentious darkness over your heads, will often come under the serious consideration of the Council in Zion; and your humble servant will not be forgetful to plead your cause in that Council where he has for years had the honor to act a humble part. Your kindness to me during my residence among you will not only oblige me to be your unflinching friend in Zion, but continually enhance my delight in contributing my best efforts for your well-being to the day of my death. I have endeavored during my presidency among you, to treat all Saints without partiality or hypocrisy, and with courtesy and unfeigned love. And your reciprocal bearing towards me has embalmed you in my memory so long as truth and gratitude are my light and my way-mark.

"If I have erred in discipline, I think it has been on the side of excessive forbearance. The cloak of charity has sometimes been stretched in order to hide folly and save a soul from death.

"It has been my happy lot to see the British churches enjoy great prosperity in the most exciting and eventful part of the nineteenth century. Famine and cholera, insurrection and revolution, and depression of trade, have paralyzed the growth of the sectarian churches; but the power of godliness has been strikingly manifest in the enlargement of the Kingdom of God and His Saints. About 10,000 have been added to Christ by baptism, and nearly 30,000 souls have been brought to adhere to the Kingdom of God during the last two years. The Presidents of conferences and Priesthood generally, have wrought diligently and in perfect union with counsel, and the result has been a great harvest of souls. With little exception, I have never had occasion to reprove a President of a conference, but their co-operation with me has been spontaneous, free, and liberal; and I have the satisfaction to add that my own labors have received the explicit approbation of the first

Presidency in Zion, by whose faith and prayers in common with those of all Saints, I have been continually sustained, and trust in God that I shall be able to stand without rebuke unto the end, through your faith and prayers in my behalf. The fellowship of the Saints is better to me than gold and silver; and a good name among the faithful is more precious than rubies. Better may I sleep untimely in death than forfeit the confidence of those who are faithful and chosen.

"Beloved Saints, suffer a little exhortation before I leave you. Keep the fellowship of the faithful, lest being alone you are beguiled from your steadfastness in Christ, and are cast out with the fearful and unbelieving. Let not the things that you cannot understand prevent you from maintaining, unitedly with your brethren the truths that you do understand.

"Walk in the light so far as you comprehend it, and you will never be in darkness—worlds without end. Keep your bodies in subjection to the law of righteousness, lest being defiled you become a prey to Satan. While there is a great prize before you worthy of your loftiest ambition, strive for it, but strive 'lawfully.' What is lawful for one, is not necessarily so for another. Let every man walk in his own light and not in another's. The spirit is given to every man to profit withal, and the spirit will not lead men to commit folly and wickedness, or indulge in surfeiting and drunkenness, or wantonness, envy, and evil surmising.

"The Spirit will not lead men to condemn a matter or principle in contrariety to those who are set in the Church to perfect it. Seducing spirits will be let loose in order to sift men as wheat, practicing all deceivableness of unrighteousness in and through them that perish.

"Beware of such, for their reward is from beneath. Rest assured, also, that sincerity alone is no proof of rectitude. Persons who have a standing in the church may be deeply and truly sincere, while they are at the same time rotten with the spirit of apostasy. The engine of sincerity may drag the car of ignorance, blindness, and self-righteousness into the abyss of destruction. The doctrine of devils are destined, before many years shall pass away, to be confirmed by lying wonders; and the false miracles of 'the beast' will bewilder and confound those who know not God and obey not His Gospel. * * *

"Brethren farewell. That grace, mercy, and peace may be multiplied unto you all, through Jesus Christ, is the prayer of

"Your humble servant,

"ORSON SPENCER."

* * *

CHAPTER XI.

FATHER'S RETURN.

IT would be utterly impossible for me to describe the gladness which filled the hearts of my brothers and sisters and myself, when the welcome news reached us that our father was coming home with a company of emigrants and would be here by the latter part of September, 1849. As the time drew near we anxiously awaited his coming, and finally the day was set that he was expected to arrive.

We were very happy that day, and counted the hours, until evening set in, still no father came. Finally thinking he would not come until the next day, we went to bed, but not to sleep, for we felt the disappointment so keenly.

All at once the sound of wheels was heard and in listening we noticed that they stopped at our gate. We were up in an instant, when a man came to the door and inquired if we knew where Dr. Richards lived. I was thrown off my guard entirely and began telling him the direction to take, but Ellen who had been listening to his step and voice, said, "Pa, is that you?" He then made himself known, for it was indeed our dear father, who had been belated and used this little ruse, to see if we would know him. We were in the dark when he came to the door and it was amusing to hear sister Lucy, who was seven years old, caper around on the bed in high glee, until the candle was lit, and then see her curl up in the corner and not say a word.

Oh! what a joyful time, to see the only parent we had, after so long an absence. Father did not look very natural, for he had always worn spectacles when at home; but while in England he had a severe spell of sickness, and upon recovering, his eyesight returned to him, so that he never needed to wear glasses again. This made him look a little odd to us. He explained that the company would not be in until tomorrow, he having come ahead in a one horse buggy. The next day we were introduced to our new mother, Martha Knight Spencer, and little sister Martha who was nearly two years old, and a lovely child. I can imagine how new and strange everything must have appeared to my stepmother, in leaving England for a home in Utah, where we had to live in one little room, and sleep in wagons until father could build, which he did the same fall. The English saints who came with my father were very nice people. They soon went to other settlements, mostly to Big Cottonwood, making homes there.

The next spring Ellen was married to Hiram B. Clawson, on the 18th of March. The following winter father was appointed Chancellor of the University of Deseret, which school was held in the building known as the Council House, located opposite the south-east corner of the Temple Block. He was principal of the school, assisted by Judge W. W. Phelps. That was the last school I ever attended.

※ ※ ※

CHAPTER XII.

MARRIAGE AND HOME IN FARMINGTON.

On the 27th of March, 1851, I was married to Thomas Rogers. And the ensuing week we moved to Farmington, Davis Co., sixteen miles north of Salt Lake City, which has been my home ever since. We were among the early settlers, there being only a few families scattered here and there, upon our arrival. I remember how lovely and romantic the place looked, with high mountains on the east and the Great Salt Lake on the west.

A new life was opening up before me. I was just merging from girlhood into womanhood, being in my seventeenth year. I little realized the care and responsibility of looking after a home of my own. Like many other new beginners, there was nothing for me but the bright side to look upon, and I imagined myself equal to the emergency. To show you the contrast between the times then and now, I will give a description, in part, of my house and furniture. We moved into a log house with two rooms, the door of the one used as a kitchen, faced west, and as the house was built on a rise of ground, we had a good view of the lake in the distance. A pure stream of water ran by the foot of the hill below, and instead of having a well close to the house, every pail of water that was used had to be carried up this hill. The roof of our house was made of willows and dirt, as shingles were not very plentiful. My best room had two six lighted windows; the floor was covered with home made carpet, given to us by my husband's mother. In those days there were no lovely bed-room sets, which were both useful and ornamental, but the furniture in general was rather of a makeshift sort, and different things were invented for convenience, among which was the toilet. The one I owned was made by boring two auger holes in one of the logs of the house, then driving in pegs strong enough to hold up a dry goods box. This box I covered with a white cloth, hanging a curtain around the outside, so that no one could see the treasures kept underneath, which treasures consisted mostly of clean clothes after they had been ironed and put away. On the top of this toilet I put some choice books, besides some presents and other notions, which were in time badly soiled for want of a better place. The kitchen had an immense jam. In the fire place was a crane with hooks to hang kettles on, andirons to hold up the wood, a shovel and pair of tongs with brass knobs, a bake kettle and skillet, to bake bread and pies. Stoves were scarce in those days, but as I had always been used to one, the cooking was quite a trial to me, especially in baking custards and puddings, for they spilled so easily, and many a cry I used to have over my fancied poor success in cooking. None of our furniture was painted, therefore once or twice a week I had four chairs, a table, and cupboard, besides the floor to scour. Having no scrubbing brush I had to use sand and a cloth. I must not forget to mention that my cupboard was filled with lovely china dishes; a present from my father, which china he had brought with him from England.

When my broom gave out and it was not convenient to send to the city for a new one I would go to the brook and get some nice willows that grew on the bank and use them as a substitute. With all these little hindrances in housekeeping, I would not like the reader to imagine that I was unhappy; far from it; with the exception of certain times of trial, some of which have been mentioned, "I was happy as a bird." Our coming to Farmington was through my husband's step-father, Andrew L. Lamoreaux, who had a share in a mill situated at the mouth of the canyon, about half a mile from where we lived; as his family was not living there at the time, he wished us to move up so he could board with us. He was one of the best men I ever became acquainted with, and I loved him next to my own father.

Mother Lamoreaux and her youngest son, Willie, aged five years, were with us most of the time for the first two weeks. It may be necessary to explain a little before proceeding farther. When my husband was about a year old, his parents, Archibald and Isabella Rogers, emigrated to America and settled in Canada. In the course of time three daughters were added to the family.

The father had not enjoyed good health for a few years previous, and finally died, not having the privilege of hearing Mormonism.

Later on Mrs. Rogers made the acquaintance of Andrew L. Lamoreaux, to whom she was subsequently married. They had joined the Church of Jesus Christ of Latter-day Saints, and were partakers in some of the many trials that came upon the Saints; were in Kirtland, and present at the dedication of the first temple reared to the Most High in these latter days. They had kept with the Church in their journeyings, and at the time of my marriage were living in Salt Lake City. As I stated previously, Brother

Lamoreaux, having an interest in the mill at Farmington, boarded with us.

We had good neighbors, which made it very pleasant for me. Brother Daniel Miller's family lived a little northwest of us, while Brother Thomas Smith's folks lived on the South.

Then, over by the mill was Brother Lyman Hinman's family, who had been intimate friends of my parents; also Brother David Lamoreaux, who lived at the mill.

On Sunday we went to meeting, which was held in a log room, used both for a meeting-house and school purposes. In a few months my husband bought a farm close by what was afterward the town site of Farmington. The next spring a log house was built sixteen by fourteen feet. In this house my eldest son, Orson, was born.

When my babe was six weeks old I had an attack of sickness which began with a terrible distress in my stomach, spells of which I have been subject to ever since, causing me to have poor health the greater part of my life.

About this time, Andrew Lamoreaux was sent

on a mission to France, the land of his fathers. In three years time he was released to come home, but did not live to reach his destination, for upon arriving in St. Louis he took the cholera and died, in a house owned by Brother James H. Hart.

In the summer of 1852, my father, in company with Brother Jacob Houtz, went on a mission to Prussia. But the ruling authorities there would not let them preach, and banished them immediately; threatening their lives if they failed to go. They managed to circulate a few tracts secretly, but were warned in a dream to leave, so they took their departure for England, where they labored in the ministry, returning to Utah in the summer of 1853. A short time before father started on that mission, I made a visit to the city, and after having supper at mother Lamoreaux's, went over home, (as I always called it), in the evening. There I found that father was blessing his children. It seemed providential, for I had come just in time to take my turn. Hiram Clawson was acting as scribe, so the blessings were written down, and a copy was given to me afterward, which has been a great comfort to me in connection with my patriarchal blessings.

※ ※ ※

CHAPTER XIII.

MY FATHER'S LAST MISSION—LETTERS TO HIS FAMILY.

In 1854, father was called upon to take another mission to the United States of America. His health was not very good at the time, but he did not complain, and as on former occasions felt willing to do all he could for the Gospel's sake. I will copy from letters written by him to his wives and children; (for he had married two more wives, Margaret Miller and Jane Davis; and other children had been born to him.) These extracts will further show his faithfulness to God, his affection for his family and how willing he was to lay down his life if necessary, in the cause of Christ.

LETTER I.

INDEPENDENCE, Mo. AUG. 23, 1854.

MY EVER DEAR FAMILY: Last evening I arrived here, after a journey of forty-five days across the plains. I am well and very thankful to God, my Heavenly Father, for his guardian care over me and the little company with me. Elder —— proposed at the beginning of the journey that we all take turns standing guard at night. I told them that I was willing to take my equal share, and I thought that God, whom I seek to serve with a perfect heart and a willing mind, would give me all necessary strength to do it. I prayed that He would do so most fervently, and surely He has done what I asked Him to do. When I have stood guard every third or fourth night, it has given me a sweet opportunity to meditate and call upon my great Father in Heaven to bless me and to bless my mission; to bless my wives and all my dear children, my animals, my fields, and my gardens. I have long and greatly desired an opportunity to commune with my God, and my own heart, and thoroughly examine myself and see whether I have much or little faith. Hence my watch-nights have rarely seemed long to me. You know how busy I used to be at home, and how thoughtful; but now I have had a good chance to ask your dear husband and father about his faith and his hope, and whether he could give up all—his dear family and life even for the Gospel.

O! I have seen myself to be very small and entirely dependent before the searching gaze of God's eye; but I feel to hold fast to the Lord with a stronger grasp than ever. My continued and never failing cry to Him is, by night and by day, 'O! Lord keep my heart from all error and deception and transgression lest I fall as many other men and woman also have done.' Then my heart goes out in strong desires that He will also keep my dear wives and children that I may bring them all into the celestial kingdom with me. * * * I hope you will pray mightily for me as I do for you, that our hearts may be so pure, that the evil one nor cunning men and women cannot deceive us at anytime. * * *

Tomorrow is the 24th of August; the day I reached my home in Salt Lake, one year ago. Then, when I entered the Valley, I said in my heart, shall I find my family all alive and well? will they greet me fondly, shall I find them living in peace and union? One year has rolled away and I find myself far away again among strangers; no fond looks to greet me, no soft hands to sooth my brow, or to put the pillow under my head when I lie down to rest. All right, a better time is coming.   *   *   *

"Your ever loving husband and father
"ORSON SPENCER."

EXTRACTS.

CINCINNATI, Nov. 18th 1854.

*   *   *   I never felt more deeply and constantly the necessity of feeling habitually penitent, humble, and diligent, in order to learn the way of eternal life, I have realized to some happy extent, the fulfillment of the blessings pronounced by Brothers Hyde and Woodruff upon my head. I see that all past attainments look very small and I truly abhor myself because I am so imperfectly fitted to glorify Him who is so rich in mercy to me. I daily and hourly hope to please my Heavenly Father better than I have in times past. Can I but become pure in heart, I have the immutable promise that I shall see God and come back into His presence and be acknowledged among His worthy sons. This pleasing hope makes me contented with my mission, and my absence from you and others that I love. I know that my Heavenly Father wants me to exercise unwavering faith in Him with all my heart. But still I learn slowly and am even slower to practice. But it appears to me I do strive more diligently, and constantly than ever I did before, both to know and do the will of my Father in Heaven. I would not ask Him to let me go home or lessen my privations unless he should see it to be for my good. I have realized that I never can be truly happy only in doing His will, even though it be unto death. Herein is the true happiness, riches, honor and eternal glory of the Saints. I don't want my dear, precious family to pray for me to come home, unless my Heavenly Father shall be pleased with my return; but pray that I may know to a certainty what the will of the Lord is, and joyfully and thankfully do it. I am very anxious to publish a paper here if it should be wisdom; but Elder Snow's counsel has delayed me, and now Elder Taylor and Elder Snow wish me to join and help them start their paper, and then they tell me that they will give me a lift towards starting mine. At present there is nobody here to help me start a paper, nor even to pay my board; but still I hope to overcome all difficulties and get out a monthly periodical before long. I am in no way discouraged, although the Lord has taken peace from the earth and withdrawn His spirit from the inhabitants; yet the hearts and destinies are all in His hands, and He can and will accomplish all His designs.

"There is a little band of Saints here, some few of them begin to show the fondness and friendship of the Saints. When I got back from St. Louis last night, several young Saints that I baptized had a little race to see who should shake hands with me first. This seemed a little like old times in England; some of the same wept when they saw me going away to St. Louis. The Lord always has raised up friends for me, and if I am faithful He always will do it in times to come.   *   *   *

"Orson Spencer."

* * * I have been much blessed with the revelations of the Holy Comforter, opening the eyes of my understanding as they have never before been opened. The Lord has enabled me to call Him Father with a greater joy, and a greater assurance than ever before. I have seen the folly of earthly wisdom, and tasted the true word of God with more satisfaction than ever before. And it is the Lord alone that has done it. And I marvel that He has done it unto me, while so many millions of people have not tasted the power of the worlds to come. It is this that makes me peaceful and happy though in the midst of the wicked, and far away from the objects of my love.   *   *   *

"I am daily looking for letters from you. Although I am well contented with my mission, and particular allotment, still neither my mission nor my religion forbid me to indulge occasionally in fond and tender recollections of my home and the beloved ones that dwell there; no, far from it. The Gospel sanctifies the affections of husbands and wives and of parents and children, and makes those affections purer and stronger and more abiding; it enables us to contemplate the wide, endless, and soul enrapturing consequences of conjugal ties. And we are separated, too, for a little season, in order that we may better understand each other's value, and love more fervently and serve one another more patiently.

"When we have proved one another in prosperity and adversity, in a time of absence and also of presence—in a time when we are spoken evil of, and when we are spoken well of, then if we are found true to God and our covenants, nothing can separate us from God, or from each other. Such a trial and probation is necessary for both husbands and wives, in order that they may know each other, and rejoice over each other. My never ceasing prayer to God is that we may be kept steadfast, and true to all that will qualify us to have part with the faithful sons and daughters in the first resurrection. I continually strive to come up to the spirit of my mission, and to fulfill all the designs of all those who sent me. This is a reigning object with me daily, and although you may be comfortably situated at home, still I realize that you have some trials and probably some temptations, yet through faithfulness the Lord will deliver you out of them all; and that which you most desire in meekness and contrition of spirit you will realize. But the God of all the earth, even our Father in Heaven, will confer His favors only in His own time and way. Holy men and women in all ages have always had to wait, in order to get His favors, and such as He has loved most He has also stretched their faith, and patience to the utmost, before He would confer the desired blessings. The unity and peace that is in your family and habitation show to me that the Lord is with you, and does pour out His blessings upon you. You all speak well of each other, and this is a good sign that the spirit of God abides with you. I suppose that you have no tattling visitors to carry mischief to and from your habitation. * * *

"My health is good, and I try to keep it so. I spend considerable time in writing, some of which is published in Elder Snow's paper, and some in Elder Taylor's. Some time is used in visiting, and some in reading, etc. Now I bless you once more and say farewell."

"Your ever affectionate husband and father,
"ORSON SPENCER."

ST. LOUIS, JULY 17th, 1855.

* * * "My own health has not been first-rate for a few weeks past; still, I expect it to be better, and hope that my journey to the Cherokee nation will improve it. The climate here is hot and sultry and rather unhealthy to my frame; but when cold weather comes I hope to be strong and lively again. My feelings are good and cheerful, and I rejoice much in my mission to the states, as I have in all my missions that were ever given me in the church. I feel thankful that Brother Brigham has counted me worthy to be entrusted with such an important mission as that of visiting the Cherokee people.

I hope and pray continually that much good will result from it. I rejoice that such a mighty effort is being made to instruct the various tribes. It seems to be just the right time to visit the red men, and a critical time too, for all people, red and white, saints and gentiles. But people are beginning to see and feel that the Mormons are in the best condition of anybody, and the most likely to have peace, and union and prosperity. They are also afraid of our growing power and importance among the nations. I am well satisfied that the missions to the United States have done a great amount of good. They cannot publish anything against us, or contrive any plots to persecute us, but they find the Mormon Elders and their publications greatly in their way. Our church in Cincinnati numbers over one hundred members and is in a prosperous condition at present.

"I expect to remain in St. Louis, after my Cherokee mission terminates, until Elder Snow returns or until otherwise disposed of by President Young. Your letters breathe a most kind and excellent spirit. The good feelings which exist between you all in the family assure me that the Lord is with you and will be while you love one another and strive for peace. * * * How happy is that person who has one true friend, and how much more happy those who can call a large multitude their friends, true unto death, bound together in one everlasting covenant, never to be broken. Such a people is my people and the God of such a people is my God for ever. Let me die many deaths before I turn away from such a God or from such a people; and whatever there is in my disposition or habits that does not harmonize with such a glorious people, I pray fervently that it may be altered and put away, until I am one with the faithful saints, and love those who love God and His priesthood.

"I am surprised to find my sheet almost full, while there are many things of family matters, etc., that I want to say. I feel to bless you, and hope that you will have many things next winter that will make you comfortable."

"With undying love,
"Your affectionate husband,
"ORSON SPENCER."

The next news we received from father was written by another than his dear hand; and told us of his being attacked with a severe illness, from which he never recovered. For particulars of his death I will copy part of an obituary from the Millennial Star, and finish from one written at St. Louis.

※ ※ ※

CHAPTER XIV.

DEATH OF ELDER ORSON SPENCER.

FROM THE MILLENNIAL STAR.

* * * * * * *

Another of the mighty men of Israel has fallen. Elder Orson Spencer departed this life at three o'clock a. m., on Monday, Oct. 15, 1855, in the city of St. Louis; after an illness of forty days.

* * * His parents belonged to that virtuous, industrious class of New Englanders of the Puritan stock, which has produced so many eminent men to figure on the stage of action in all the various departments of life.   *   *   *

At the age of fifteen, he entered the academy at Lenox, in his native country, where he received the highest honors of his class. There, at a public examination, the high sheriff of the county, Henry C. Brown noticed his unusual proficiency, and ascertaining that his father was in very moderate circumstances, voluntarily offered to loan the necessary means for his education, and wait until he could pay it, after its completion. He entered Union College, state of New York, in 1819, and graduated with great honor in 1824. The next year he obtained a situation as teacher in an academy in Washington, Wilkes Co., Georgia. In addition to the duties of his calling, he turned his attention to the study of law. About that time, he had some singular manifestations on the subject of religion and soon after joined the Baptist Church, and left the study of law for that of theology. He entered the Theological College at Hamilton, State of New York, where he graduated in 1829. He labored in the ministry about twelve years,

and received the Gospel of Jesus Christ in 1841.
* * *

He presided over the British Mission and ably edited the Millennial Star about two years. During his ministry here, he wrote the most of a series of letters to the Rev. Mr. Crowel, which were embodied and published as Spencer's Letters. * * * * *

FROM THE ST. LOUIS LUMINARY.

It becomes our melancholy duty to announce the decease of our well beloved brother Orson Spencer, late Editor of the Luminary, and President of the Church of Jesus Christ of Latter-day Saints in the Ohio and Mississippi valleys. * * * He died without a groan or struggle and could hardly be said to have tasted the pangs of death. Peace and serenity have characterized his whole life, and were manifestly enjoyed during his illness, and sealed and engraven upon his placid countenance in the hour of death; and all who saw him felt to wish that their life might be the life of the righteous, and their last end like his. It will be remembered that some time in July, or early in August, 1854, our deceased brother left his home in Salt Lake City, being appointed by the First Presidency on a mission to Cincinnati, where he remained until July, 1855, when he was sent for by President Erastus Snow to take the editorial chair of the Luminary; he lost no time but left his field of labor immediately, and arrived in St. Louis on the 7th of July, and was forthwith installed in that position, which he filled with so much ease and dignity. He remained but a very short time in this city, being called to go on a mission to the Cherokee Nation. He started July 21, and remained in the camp at Atchison until the last company of the emigration had taken up their line of march for the valley, when, in company of Elder James McGaw, on the 5th of August, he proceeded on his mission to the Cherokee Nation; where he remained until the 5th of September, when, having completed his mission and finding himself attacked with fever accompanied with chills, which prevailed in the Nation at that time, he returned immediately to St. Louis, where he arrived on the 17th of September, fatigued, debilitated, and afflicted. For about ten days after his return he was subject to the chills and fever with more or less intensity, and when finally broken up the disease assumed a mild stage of typhoid fever, and the general symptoms discoverable through his illness were torpidity, lassitude, and debility, from which he found it impossible to rally. He was attended during his illness by Dr. White of this city, and later by Dr. Clinton of Philadelphia, who was sent for expressly to attend him. The Doctor arrived here on Thursday, the 11th inst. He found Brother Spencer in the very last stage of his illness; he had that morning given up hopes of life, and had resigned himself, and committed his family into the hands of the Lord. When he first saw Brother Clinton he felt revived and encouraged, and almost sorry he had shown signs of weakness in giving up. But notwithstanding he was so anxious to see the Doctor, and expressed such faith in his prescriptions and ministrations, no inducements were sufficient to get him to take anything calculated to restore him. He therefore gradually declined and finally expired, fully satisfied with life, and rejoicing in the hope of glory beyond the tomb. Dr. Clinton had no hope for his recovery from the first. It appeared evident that his earthly course was run and that he had finished the work given him to do and he could say with full assurance, "I have fought the good fight, finished my course and kept the faith, henceforth there is laid up for me a righteous crown which God, the righteous judge, will give unto me, and not to me only, but unto all who love His appearing."

Between three and four o'clock on Tuesday afternoon, the brethren and sisters commenced to gather around the house of Brother Swales—where the remains of our respected brother lay awaiting interment—anxious to obtain a last look at him they so much loved, and when Dr. Clinton stood o'er the lifeless form, after addressing the mournful spectators in praise of the noble and generous character of the deceased, he fixed his eyes upon him, and exclaimed pathetically: "Brother Orson, farewell; we shall soon meet with you again." Every heart responded to the sentiment, "Amen!" The scene was solemn and imposing. The Doctor's heart was too full for further utterance, and he was relieved by Brother John Banks, who offered to our Father in Heaven a most beautiful and appropriate prayer. Soon after four o'clock the funeral procession was seen moving towards the cemetery, where, after a short address from Elder James H. Hart, the earthly tabernacle of our brother was interred (for a season) with a sure and certain hope of a resurrection to eternal life. Although but little notice had been given, and consequently but little opportunity offered the Saints to prepare, yet there were not fewer than twenty, or twenty-two carriages, filled with brethren and sisters who followed the remains of Brother Spencer to their temporary resting place, as a last token of esteem and affection. * * *

The next summer my father's body was taken up and sent on to the valley, and interred in the cemetery of Salt Lake City.

The hardest thing for me to bear, was the thought of my father dying away from home, with none of his family near to comfort him in his last moments; although he had kind friends to minister to his wants, which was quite a satisfaction.

My father could be counted as one who had left father and mother, wives and children and all that he held dear, for the gospel's sake.

On the 15th of November, following, my sister Catharine was married to Brigham Young, Junior. It was one month to the day since my father had died, but as yet no word had reached us to that effect; it being impossible for the mail coaches to travel a thousand miles in so short a time. Another full month passed before the sad news came.

It seems appropriate to here insert those immortal lines of E. R. Snow's, entitled

"EVENING THOUGHTS,

OR

WHAT IT IS TO BE A SAINT."

Suggested on reading Orson Spencer's first letter in the series known as "Spencer's Letters."

"My heart is fixed—I know in whom I trust.
'Twas not for wealth—'twas not to gather heaps
Of perishable things—'twas not to twine

Around my brow a transitory wreath,
A garland deck'd with gems of mortal praise,
That I forsook the home of childhood; that
I left the lap of ease—the halo rife
With friendship's richest soft and mellow tone,
Affection's fond caresses, and the cup
O'er flowing with the sweets of social life,
With high refinement's golden peals enriched.

Ah no! a holier purpose fir'd my soul—
A nobler object prompted my pursuit:
Eternal prospects open'd to my view
And hope celestial in my bosom glowed.

God who commanded Abraham to leave
His native country, and to offer up
On the lone altar where no eye beheld
But that which never sleeps, an only son,
Is still the same; and thousands who have made
A covenant with Him by sacrifice,
Are bearing witness to the sacred truth,
Jehovah speaking has revealed His will.

The proclamation sounded in my ear—
It reached my heart—I listened to the sound,
Counted the cost, and laid my earthly all
Upon the altar; and with purpose fix'd
Unalterably, while the spirit of
Elijah's God within my bosom reigns,
Embraced the "Everlasting Covenant;"
And am determined now to be a Saint,

And number'd with the tried and faithful ones
Whose race is measured with their life; whose prize
Is everlasting, and whose happiness
Is God's approval; and to whom 'tis more
Than meat and drink to do His righteous will.

It is no trifling thing to be a Saint
In very deed—to stand upright, nor bow,
Nor bend beneath the weighty pressure of
Oppressiveness: to stand unscath'd amid
The bellowing thunders and the raging storm
Of persecution, when the hostile pow'rs
Of darkness stimulate the hearts of men
To warfare: to besiege, assault, and, with
The heavy thunderbolts of Satan, aim
To overthrow the kingdom God has rear'd.—
To stand unmov'd upon the with'ring rock
Of vile apostasy, when men depart
From the pure principles of righteousness—
Those principles requiring man to live
By every word proceeding from the mouth
Of God: to stand unwavering, undismay'd,
And unseduc'd, when the base hypocrite
Whose deeds take hold on hell, whose face is garbed
With saintly looks, drawn out by sacrilege
From the profession, but assum'd and thrown
Around him for a mantle to enclose
The black corruption of a putrid heart.
To stand on virtue's lofty pinnacle
Clad in the heav'nly robes of innocence,

Amid that worse than every other blast—
The blast that strikes at moral character,
With floods of falsehood foaming with abuse.—
To stand with nerve and sinew firmly steel'd,
When in the trying scale of rapid change,
Thrown face to face and side by side with that
Foul hearted spirit, blacker than the soul
Of midnight's darkest shade—the traitor,
The vile wretch that feeds his sordid selfishness
Upon the peace and blood of innocence;
The faithless, rotten hearted wretch, whose tongue
Speaks words of trust and fond fidelity,
While treachery, like a viper, coils behind
The smile that dances in his evil eyes:
To pass the fiery ordeal, and to have
The heart laid open, all its contents strew'd
Before the bar of strictest scrutiny:
To have the finest heart-strings drawn unto
Their utmost length, to prove their texture:
T'abide, with principle unchanged, the rack
Of cruel, torturing circumstances, which
Ride forth on revolution's blustering gale.

But yet, altho' to be a Saint, requires
A noble sacrifice— an arduous toil—
A persevering aim; the great reward
Awaiting the grand consummation will
Repay the price, however costly; and
The pathway of the Saint the safest path
Will prove; tho' perilous: for 'tis foretold,

All things that can be shaken, God will shake.
Kingdoms and governments and institutes,
Both civil and religious, must be tried—
Tried to the core, and sounded to the depth.

Then let me be a Saint, and be prepar'd
For the approaching day, which like a snare
Will soon surprise the hypocrite—expose
The rottenness of human schemes—shake off
Oppressive fetters—break the gorgeous reins
Usurpers hold, and lay the pride of man,—
The pride of nations low in dust."

* * *

CHAPTER XV.

A FEW MONTHS IN SALT LAKE CITY

Grasshopper War—A Trip to Big Cottonwood Canyon.

My second child, Andrew Lo'ce (we call him Locy), was born in Salt Lake City, Dec. 19, 1854. He was named for Andrew L. Lamoreaux, whose mother's maiden name was Lo'ce, which is French. My husband had engaged to assist in herding some stock, on what was called the range, some miles above Farmington; therefore I was taken to the city for a few months, and lived with Mother Lamoreaux, who gave me the best of care, assisted by her daughters, Mary and Caroline. My husband's family were all as good and kind to me as my own sisters could be; and when my health was poor, one of the girls would come and help me with my work. A married sister, Mrs. Isabel Sewell, came one time and nursed me. Another sister, Mrs. Ann Dewey, who was a milliner, often helped me with a hat or bonnet free of charge, which was duly appreciated.

Early in the spring we returned to Farmington, living through the summer with Edwin and Ann Walker, their house being only a short distance from ours, and thus our two small families were company for each other.

A town had been laid out, and my husband having taken a lot, he built an adobe house with two rooms. We moved in before they were finished, but were happy to be under the shelter of a shingle roof, this being the first time we had owned such a luxury. In our log cabins every time after a hard rain we would have a certain amount of plaster to clean up, so of course we appreciated the change.

In the summer of 1855, grasshoppers came in swarms, destroying the crops and gardens. They took us by surprise at first, but finally the people rallied and waged war with the enemy; ditches were dug, into which the grasshoppers were driven, and afterwards covered with dirt or drowned with water. Still they came and swept the land, till scarcely a vestige of anything green could be seen; at times they were so thick in the air that we could hardly see the sun. This caused much suffering. Flour was scarce, and many of the people lived on bran bread. My husband sold a horse for $20, with which he bought a little flour; but for a short time we fared no better than those who lived on the bran diet.

Having a desire to assist my husband, and being handy at cutting and fitting dresses, I used to take in sewing, which was done by hand, as there were no sewing machines in Farmington at that time. I also taught school two or three terms in my own house. The grasshoppers came again the next year, but did not do so much damage.

On the 24th of July, 1857, when my third child, Ella, was a little over three weeks old, there was an excursion to Big Cottonwood Canyon, which is twelve miles below Salt Lake City; but the excursionists had to go about ten miles up the canyon before they arrived at the place appointed for their day's enjoyment. My husband was called to go as one of the guards, or minute men. A company of these men had been selected from different settlements, and they were expected to be ready at a moment's warning, as there was often trouble with the Indians. This made it necessary for them to have their clothing and firearms in readiness. President Young, and quite a company from Salt Lake City, were going on this excursion, my sisters being among the number; also some of our neighbors in Farmington were going. This made me have a desire to go too. So, not listening to the advice of those having better judgment, who said my babe was too young, I went along, leaving my little boys in the care of Sister Knowles.

Thinking there would be very little to do, I supposed it would be nice to ride up there and back; but having to travel over some pretty rough road, the jolting of the wagon affected me, and by the time we got half-way up the canyon, where we camped for the night, I felt quite sick, and repented having left home; but it was too late to think of returning. With the kind care of Sisters Sariah Tyler and Ann Walker, who camped with us, I got along very well; felt much better the next day, and enjoyed in a measure the beautiful scenery at the top of the mountains, or rather the little basin of land among the crags that had been chosen for the occasion. In this basin there was a lake, where many of the excursionists went fishing, while others took walks through the hills or engaged in the dance. On the 25th all returned to their homes in safety.

It was that Twenty-fourth, while in the tops of the mountains, that President Young received word that a company of soldiers called Johnson's Army, were on the road to Utah, with the intention of killing the Mormon men and occupying their homes. President Young prophesied in the name of the Lord that they would never enter the Valley of the Great Salt Lake until the Latter-day Saints permitted them to. His words were fulfilled, for the army was kept in the mountains all winter. Our men were interspersed through the canyons and ravines, and their numbers were perhaps magnified in the eyes of the enemy, as in days of old, when the Lord made a few men to appear like a multitude. The soldiers of the army were afraid to come any farther, and it was learned afterward that many of them suffered from cold and hunger. President Young, hearing that they had no salt, sent them some from Salt Lake, which they refused at first, but finally took it, as there was no other chance of getting any. My husband and many others were in the mountains standing guard in their turn from the middle of August until January, when they returned home.

CHAPTER XVI.

SALMON RIVER TRAGEDY.—THE MOVE SOUTH.

In March, 1858, word came to us that the Indians had made a raid on the settlers at Salmon River (at a place over 400 miles north of Farmington,) and that help was needed immediately. Some two years previous a few families from Farmington had been sent there to make a settlement, with Brother Thomas Smith as president of the mission. They were living in a fort which they had built to protect themselves from the Indians, who at this particular time were quite hostile. The Indians in trying to steal and drive off the stock of the settlers (which they succeeded in doing) killed two men, George McBride and James Miller, and wounded six others, namely, Thomas Smith, Oliver Robinson, Andrew Quigley, Fountain Welch, Orson Rose, and a man by the name of Shurtliff. The Indians had surrounded the fort, and for days the inmates lived in fear of their lives, not knowing what the end might be. Yet by watching their opportunity, two men managed to leave the fort in the night and go for help. Traveling day and night, they only stopped to rest their horses until they reached the settlements of our people. My husband was among the number who went to their assistance. The families were moved back to their former homes, and the mission was broken up. It was never President Young's way to encourage hostile measures with the Lamanites, but to show them the better way of life by treating them with forbearance and brotherly kindness. He therefore considered it best to recall those whom he had sent there, and wait a more favorable time for building up that portion of the country.

Soon after that, negotiations were entered into by the leaders of our people and the officers of Johnson's Army, by which the soldiers were allowed to pass through Salt Lake City and camp in the western part of the valley. Not knowing how well they would carry out the treaty, President Young sent word to all the northern settlements of Utah to gather up their effects and move to the south. By the middle of May every town and village north, and nearly all the homes in Salt Lake City, were vacated. A few men were left to stand guard and to apply the torch to their houses if necessary; for they had made preparations to burn their dwellings rather than let their enemies inhabit them. Never was such a thing known in modern history, such union among a people in listening to the call of one man. But this was by reason of the same Spirit inspiring the people of God as that by which His Prophet spoke. The sheep knew the voice of the good shepherd.

The sacrifice was made and accepted of God. The people were saved through faith and their obedience to counsel.

Our family went as far as Springville, fifty-six miles from Salt Lake City, and camped on a lot owned by John Pine. His family were very kind indeed; they gave us vegetables, and helped us in different ways. It was the same throughout the entire community; there was a general feeling to assist.

In the meantime the army came into the valley, passed through Salt Lake City very quietly, and took up their abode west of the Jordan River and south of Salt Lake Valley, at a place called Cedar Valley. Their settlement they named Camp Floyd. Soon after the soldiers had passed through the city word was sent from head-quarters that the people were at liberty to return to their homes, which most of them did as speedily as possible.

When we arrived in Farmington, it was the very picture of a deserted village. Having been gone two months, the gardens and yards were over-run with weeds and grass. A few potatoes that had been left in our house had withered and dried up; but I soaked some of them out and cooked them. Some of the farmers had sowed considerable wheat in the spring before leaving their homes, and had returned at different times to water it, thereby saving enough for their bread.

CHAPTER XVII.

THE TRIAL OF SICKNESS AND DEATH.—WORDS OF PRES. HEBER C. KIMBALL.

My fourth child, Howard was born July 27th, 1859. He was a bright healthy baby, but was taken sick and died, when fourteen months old. I had been so happy previous to this; the trials of poverty and sickness that we had passed through were nothing compared to this great sorrow that had overtaken me; and I mourned for my babe incessantly. Perhaps being feeble in body made me feel the loss more than if I had been healthy and strong. I was ill most of the next winter, and came near to death a number of times; yet notwithstanding I longed to see my babe, I did not wish to die, but wanted to live to rear my other children, realizing what it was to be left motherless at an early age. I prayed to the Lord constantly, and told Him if He would spare my life, I would try to keep His commandments and serve Him to the best of my ability. My prayers were answered, and I lived to have eight more children, but only raised four out of the eight; therefore my life has been intermingled with joys and sorrows.

It is not necessary for me to relate all the episodes that I have passed through, but I will briefly touch upon some of the more important ones.

On the 29th of March, 1861, my son George was born. My next child Clarence, died when nineteen months old with the measles which disease at that time proved fatal to a great many of the young children in our settlement. While attending the funeral of little Clarence, Orson who was just getting over the measles, took cold in his eyes; inflammation set in, and for nearly five years he was not able to do any work when the sun shone bright, or when there was snow on the ground. This was quite a trial to us, but I had faith that some day his eyes would get well and my hopes were realized. For after a number of years, he had occasion to go to Montana as a teamster, and the change of air strengthened his sight, so that he could soon do without using glasses.

•In 1866, when my daughter Lucy was a few months old, I had occasion to go to the city; and while on my way to Brother Savage's Art gallery, where I had some business, met President Heber C. Kimball. He looked at me very sharply for a few seconds, then after shaking hands, walked with me to the gallery, talking as we went. At the door we met my sister Ellen and my brother Howard. President Kimball continued the conversation, which was mostly directed to myself. He seemed to read me like a book, and to understand my inmost thoughts. In speaking of the future, he said it was not best for us to know what was ahead of us, or we might not be able to stand; said I did not begin to know what was before me; but told me to continue as faithful as I had been, and all would be well, for there was a great work for me to do. He cautioned me about telling what I knew; said he knew things that he had never told to a living soul. He gave me good counsel and spoke words of encouragement, which sank deep into my heart, words that I have pondered over many times since and wondered what they meant.

※ ※ ※

CHAPTER XVIII.

MARRIAGE AND DEATH OF SISTER LUCY.

On the 2nd of January, 1867, my sister Lucy was married to George W. Grant, Jr. In one year from that time wanting three days, she died and was buried on the anniversary of her wedding day. Little did I think the year before, when she came up to wait upon me in my sickness, that she would be the first to go to the other side. Yet it brought to my mind a saying of my father, in one of his letters to us from England; he told Ellen that she should have the privilege of bringing Lucy up to womanhood, which was verified.

OBITUARY.

DESERET NEWS, DEC. 30, 1867.

"Died, in this city, in child bed, at noon yesterday, Lucy C. Spencer Grant, wife of Elder

George W. Grant, now south at St. Thomas on a mission.

"Sister Lucy C. Spencer was the daughter of Orson and Catharine C. Spencer. She was born October 9th, 1842 in Nauvoo, Illinois, and was at her death, twenty-five years, two months and twenty days old. Brother Orson Spencer's touching account of the circumstances under which he left Nauvoo, and the death of his beloved wife, published in his Letters, has made all the Saints familiar with his family. Every reader of those Letters has felt a great interest in his children. At the death of her mother, Lucy was very young, her oldest sister, Ellen, (Mrs. H. B. Clawson) though but a girl, acted the part of mother to her.   *   *   *

"The deceased was married to Elder George W. Grant about twelve months ago. The news of her sudden death will be a heavy shock to her husband; and also her brother George, who started for the Muddy a few weeks ago. Her death has cast a gloom over a wide circle of relatives and friends. Even now it can scarcely be realized that she has been snatched away so suddenly and unexpectedly by death. Every one who knew her might well have anticipated for her a prolonged life of happiness and usefulness. On Saturday afternoon she went out riding with her sister, Mrs. Clawson, and felt well all Saturday evening and night. Her child was born at 9 a. m. on Sunday, and still survives; but at noon she was a corpse. Her funeral will take place at 2 p. m. tomorrow, from the Thirteenth Ward Assembly Rooms, where the friends of the family are invited to attend."

Brother George Grant upon hearing the sad news of his wife's death, returned to Salt Lake City, broken hearted and lonely. He survived her only four years and a half, then passed away. Sister Lucy's babe, a little girl, named for its mother, was taken care of by her Grandmother Grant, and is still living.

CHAPTER XIX.

A TRYING ORDEAL.—MISSION OF ELDER THOMAS ROGERS TO ENGLAND.

My next child after Lucy, a little girl, died when three months old of whooping cough. The winter following, my health was worse than usual, and in the spring I passed through an ordeal that I think well to mention. The measles had broken out again in Farmington, and proved fatal to many. At that time I had a desire to go to the city and visit my sisters, and not being able to do much work at home, it was thought the change might do me good; so I went. After stopping in the city nearly two weeks, the time drew near for me to go home but I was not able to go, having been prostrated with those old distressed spells. About this time Lucy, the only child I had with me, came down with measles. It seemed she must have been exposed before leaving home; scarlet-fever set in which endangered her life. When the disease was at its height, Ellen's baby, Ivy, also came down with measles. I was the cause of all this trouble; I had brought sickness to my sister's family and could not even wait on myself or little girl. This wore on me until I was almost beside myself with grief; my mind became diseased, and I experienced the most horrible feelings imaginable. One night they thought Ivy was going to die, and if I ever prayed fervently to the Lord, it was then, that He would spare the lives of our children; but if either child was to be taken it might be mine. I could not endure the thought of my sister losing her babe, for she had already buried four children. While in the midst of this anxiety, lying on my bed, wondering if the Lord had indeed forsaken us, all at once a change came over me; everything seemed so lovely and beautiful, and I was as happy as could be for a few minutes. I saw no person, heard no voice, yet knew the Comforter was there, and accepted it as such, feeling to thank the Lord for even a glimmer of light.

The children were both spared, but the ordeal was not over. For on the 7th of April I gave birth to a son, which was premature and only lived five hours, just long enough to be named and blessed. There was not a man about the place at the time; but a child was sent out on the street to see if some one could not be found coming from Conference. My sister Catharine's husband, Brigham Young, Jr., and another brother came in time to bless my babe before it expired.

I asked sister Ellen if what I was then passing through, could be what Brother Kimball meant when he talked with me that day by the Art Gallery. She thought not.

I wish here to express my gratitude to those who have befriended me in times of sickness and sorrow. My sisters, Ellen and Catharine have acted the part of mother to me; they being better off as to this world's goods, have helped me to many needed comforts; and my brothers-in-law Hiram B. Clawson and Brigham Young, Jr., have been just as kind; for I have had occasion to stay at their houses weeks at a time, when sick or troubled, mostly at their expense, and never heard a word of complaint. They were ever ready to get anything necessary to make me comfortable.

At the time of which I have written in this chapter, my recovery was slow; but after a time I was able to return home to my family. Brother John Leavitt and Brother James T. Smith of Farmington, had both lost their wives of measles during my absence.

At the spring conference my husband had been called to go to Europe on a mission; therefore after my return home he made preparatin to leave, starting in June, 1869, in company with Brother Lot Smith, of Farmington, and my brother Howard Spencer, of Salt Lake City. My boys Orson and Lo'ce, aged seventeen and fifteen years, carried on the work of the farm, getting up the wood, etc. There was no coal to burn in those days, and all of our fuel had to be hauled by going four or five miles up the canyon. My sons generally went along with other men or boys and their teams; and sometimes when they were late getting home, I would be a little worried, but not much, for I always gave them into the hands of the Lord, and felt quite sure they would return safe at night.

The next year grasshoppers came again, and threatened to destroy the crops, but through the unceasing energy of the people and the mercies of God, a little grain was saved. We had five acres of wheat put in. This the hoppers did not disturb very much until it was headed out and being very anxious to save some of it, I went with my children every day for two weeks and drove grasshoppers, only stopping long enough to get our meals, and do other necessary work. By this means we saved twenty-four bushels of wheat, although some persons had predicted that we would not save a kernel.

After my husband arrived in Liverpool, he was appointed to labor in the Leeds branch, England. He was faithful as a missionary, and gained many friends, but as the climate did not agree with him, (after stopping one year) he was honorably released, and returned home in July, 1870.

CHAPTER XX.

DUTY AND AFFECTION OF CHILDREN—SORROW AGAIN.

In March, 1871, my son Orson was employed by the Z. C. M. I. Store, Salt Lake City. This was on the recommendation of his uncle, Hiram B. Clawson, Orson himself being unknown to the firm. As young men generally have to commence at the foot of the ladder my son was no exception to the rule, but began by driving a delivery wagon, which occupation he followed for a number of years.

Being steady in his habits, by studying nights to prepare himself for a better position, he was afterwards received into the store. Later on he traveled through the southern part of Utah, selling goods for the company.

He married a young lady from Ephraim, Sanpete County, by the name of Kate Madsen.

In the spring of '82, Spencer Clawson, son of H. B. Clawson, who was going into the mercantile business for himself, engaged Orson's services, and later admitted him as a partner in the firm.

Although settled in life, and rearing a family of his own, Orson does not forget the love and duty he has ever shown his parents, but is still thoughtful of their comfort, and always ready to help them when necessary.

At one time I had need of means to replenish my wardrobe and knew not where it was to come from.

The spirit whispered "Ask Orson for help, and he shall receive it back four-fold." Accordingly I wrote Orson a letter telling him that if he could help me to what I needed, I felt to say that he would get it back four-fold. As usual he responded by sending the things required. A few months after this, while Orson was going from the Store to his home, something lying in the road attracted his attention; he stooped down and picked up what proved to be some money tied up in a cloth.

The first thought was that a miner had dropped it, for the cloth was quite dirty. He therefore advertised it; but no owner came. When he was telling me of the "find," I asked him how much money there was. He answered "four-fold."

My other children, both boys and girls, do all in their power to make their father and mother comfortable. Lo'ce at one time came up from Arizona where he had been sent on a mission, and with the help of his brother George, made a number of trips to the canyon, and hauled out logs and wood, which were turned into means to build us a new room. And George, by working on the railroad, raised means to help furnish the room. During one of the above mentioned trips to the canyon, an incident occurred which made such an impression on my mind, that I wrote a sketch of it, and forwarded the same to *The Juvenile Instructor* for publication, a copy of which is reproduced here. The editor gave the title to my sketch:

MIRACULOUSLY SAVED.

The following is a true story, and shows that the hand of God is over those who put their trust in Him.

My two sons (both young men) went into the canyon for wood. They had loaded their carts with logs and were ready to hitch on their horses preparatory to returning home.

The cart of the elder brother was on a steep side hill, and not being in a good position for him to hitch on the team, he thoughtlessly took the blocks from under the wheels and tried to twist the tongue a little, but it would not move. He got hold of the single-tree, standing with his back down hill, and pulled quite hard, when all at once the cart started, and in an instant he was caught between the load and a stump that stood a few feet below.

The first thing he did was to call his brother, who was a short distance from the hill. He then exerted all his strength to free himself from his perilous position, but to no purpose, at the same time exclaiming: "My God! my

God! my God!" realizing that he was being crushed to death.

His brother came quickly, but could render no assistance, it being impossible, as they thought, to either unload or cut away the stump in time to save his life. And when it seemed that he could stand it no longer and that he must die, all at once he was lifted as it were by some unseen power, so that he got out perfectly easy, needing only a little help to extricate one foot which was fast.

As soon as he was clear of the load, he said "Thank God, I am free! I am free!"

He was very weak, and came near fainting, but that feeling passed off, and in a short time he was on his way home.

His injuries were not serious; his back troubled him some, and his limbs were bruised, which caused him to limp for a few days, but he was soon able to return to his work.

Words cannot express the thankfulness that I felt when they returned home and related what had occurred. The elder brother had always been prayerful, and had great faith in God.

His faith was strengthened, and he always looked upon it as being saved by a power from on high, from a dreadful death. It was also a witness to the younger brother, for when I asked him what he thought about it, he said, "Mother, some one helped him out."

My tenth child, which we named William, was born on the 31st of May, 1871, and only lived until the 17th of August, then died of cholera infantum. I had lotted so much on this child, and now he was taken; this making three children that 1 had lost in succession. Of my ten children only five remained. It seemed indeed as if my last hope was gone, as I felt that I had no health or strength to have any more family. And I almost lost faith in God; for once in my life, I even doubted the existence of a Supreme Being.

One day while reflecting on these things, one of father's letters came to my mind, wherein he said, "Trust in God though he slay you." I caught at the suggestion, which had surely been given by the Spirit of the Lord, and went to Him in prayer, asking Him to forgive me for my lack of faith, and to grant unto me strength to endure, feeling that I would put my trust in Him henceforth and forever. After this I felt better in spirit, was baptized for my health, visited some of the good sisters and found comfort in conversing with them. Subsequently, when pondering these things over, I felt that perhaps all the people of God would have to pass through certain ordeals to prove whether they would trust in Him to the end. Their condition might be likened to those clinging to the rod of iron, in the dream of Lehi, Book of Mormon, I. Nephi, 8th chapter. They could not see their way before them, but by holding fast to the Word of God, which was the interpretation of the rod of iron, they finally reached the tree of life, partook of the fruit and were happy. I felt willing to follow the counsel of my father, and was well repaid for my trust; for two more children were given me, Leone and Curtis; and since that time I have been blessed beyond my expectations.

On the 29th of November, 1871, I was chosen to fill the office of Secretary in the Relief Society of Farmington; which position I held until February, 1893.

※ ※ ※

CHAPTER XXI.

BROTHER HOWARD.

BEFORE proceeding farther with my personal account, I wish to relate a little of the experience of my two brothers, Howard and George Spencer.

Howard was one of the fearless kind of men who never think of danger, or shirking any duty. Belonging to the company of minute men spoken of previously, he was always on hand to go out with scouting parties when the Indians were troublesome, or for other causes. Under the generalship of Daniel H. Wells, and Hiram B. Clawson, in the fall of 1857, he went into the mountains to assist in keeping Johnson's Army from entering the Valley; and with the others thus engaged, shared the dangers and exposures of that memorable expedition.

In March, 1859, he was sent to Rush Valley to move some cattle from a ranch owned by Uncle Daniel Spencer and others, to another place. Some of the soldiers of Camp Floyd, were stationed near the ranch, and feeling enmity towards our people, showed their spite by killing the stock occasionally. Howard and a young man by the name of Clift, were selected to go and assist in the removal of the stock. Arriving about sundown, before eating his supper, Howard went to the corral to feed the cattle. A sergeant and some soldiers from camp came into the yard and ordered Howard to drive the cattle out. This he refused to do, saying he had been sent there to feed them, and if the stock were to be driven out they must do it themselves. At this the sergeant, who it seemed had come there for the purpose of quarrelling, raised his gun to strike. Howard seeing the movement lifted his pitchfork to parry the blow, which he saw descending upon his head; the blow came nevertheless, breaking the pitchfork handle in three pieces and crushing his skull. Howard fell insensible. The soldiers carried him into a tent close by laying his head downhill, as if he were nothing more than a log. While this was going on, Luke Johnson, a friend of ours, was in another tent, conversing with the officer in command. Hearing the commotion they went to learn what the trouble was, and saw the condition that Howard was in. Luke, seeing the blood flowing from his ears, nose and mouth, instantly raised his head, and placed him in a better position. A physician was sent for from Camp Floyd, and the wounds examined, which the doctor thought would prove fatal. A rough couch was prepared upon which the sufferer was placed; and the dear friend Luke remained with him all that night and the next day, until help came from Salt Lake City. The doctor had left some medicine which was to be given to the patient at intervals during the night. Brother Johnson being somewhat of a physician himself, examined the medicine and found poison in the mixture; he therefore threw it into the fire, substituting a soothing stimulant in its place. When the doctor called the next morning, he said the medicine had worked admirably.

I heard the particulars of this terrible affair from Brother Johnson's own lips, and the facts are as here stated.

It should be said of the officer in command that he did not sanction the outrage committed, but apparently regretted it very much and the sergeant was arrested and dealt with. When news reached the City, President Brigham Young sent his carriage and things necessary for Howard's comfort and Doctor Sprague, Uncle Daniel and my brother George, rode a distance of fifty or sixty miles, returning with the sufferer in the night; stopping on the way at Cousin Charles and Margaret Spencer's. They lived at the point of the mountain, near where Garfield, the well known bathing resort is now situated.

Howard was delirious for days after receiving the injury. The motion of the carriage coming to the city caused him great pain, and Cousin Margaret came in with him, holding his head and endeavoring to soothe his distress.

Doctors Anderson and France, of Salt Lake City, attended him, and found it necessary to perform two surgical operations, in which several pieces of bone were removed from the skull.

His mind was seriously affected for sometime and for months he was unable to leave the house. But having a strong constitution, he gradually improved, and finally regained his health.

Howard was married to Miss Louise Cross of Salt Lake City, in April, 1860.

At the time of the Civil War, 1862, a call was made by President Abraham Lincoln on President Young, for a company of one hundred men to go and protect the mail and telegraph lines east, as the Indians were causing trouble by tearing down the wires, and interfering with mail coaches. Howard enlisted and was gone three and a half months. The company traveled as far as Sweetwater Bridge, below Devil's Gate, repairing roads and putting the telegraph lines in order.

When they were about to return home, the Indians made a raid on a mountaineer's ranch near Bridger, stealing a band of their horses.

Howard and most of the company packed up on short notice, and under the command of Captain Lot Smith, with a few days' provisions started in pursuit; following the Indians as far as Snake River.

While swimming this river, one of their men by the name of Donald McNickold, was drowned. Some of their horses were also drowned. After losing the man Donald, they came down between the forks of the river, and made a raft to cross over the south fork. Before the attempt was made to cross, the boys who boarded the raft, (eight in number) took off their clothing ready to swim if occasion required. All went well until they reached the opposite shore, when suddenly the raft gave a lurch and tipped the passengers off. Lot Smith, Andrew Bigler, Seymour B. Young, James Sharp, and Howard Spencer scrambled for shore; some of their number swam back to the shore they had left, Andrew Bigler included. Relieved of its burden, the raft started down stream; when Captain Smith, afraid of losing it, jumped into the water at the risk of his life, swam to the raft, and providentially reached the other side with it in safety. Young, Sharp, and Spencer who had scrambled onto the shore after being shipwrecked, passed a terrible night among the brush and willows. Almost destitute of clothing, they were attacked by swarms of mosquitos, with no means of defence, no way of lighting a fire, and with no food to eat. In the morning they went up the river quite a distance, loosened a log, cast it afloat, and jumped aboard of it. With poles they guided it to the other shore, landing it near the camp of their companions. As the log touched the bank, Howard being on the front end and Seymour in the middle of the log both jumped off, but could not hold it until James could do likewise. The log wheeled around with Sharp on the farther end and darting into an eddy, went with the current down the river. Fortunately it struck a sandbar some distance below, and James was rescued.

The party being pretty well worn out by this time, and the Indians having gained the advantage in distance, they thought best to return. Traveling about two days' journey down the river, they crossed over on the ferry, and arrived home a used up lot of men, but thankful for their lives. This is only one of the many hardships experienced by the noble men who spent much of their time in working for the benefit of others, in the early days of Utah.

At one time Howard had occasion to go with others to Bear Lake Valley, after Chief Washokee, who was wanted at Bridger. There were no settlements in the valley at that time. In 1864, he went again with President Young and party, at which time settlers were moving in.

During the spring of '66, he with others answered a call to go to Sanpete, to protect the people from the Indians. In a fight that ensued, the company lost one man, and had some of their horses killed.

Howard took a small contract in Echo Canyon, in 1868, helping to build the Union Pacific railroad. In '69 he was called to go on a mission to England, he labored in the London Conference for about a year, returning home in 1870. Part of the years of '73 and '74 he was night watchman of Z. C. M. Institution. In the fall of '74 he was called by President Young to go to Long Valley in the southern part of Utah and preside.

The next spring the people there commenced to live in the United Order, from which the settlement derived the name of Orderville. In 1877, he again went to England, laboring in the London Conference for about two years and returning home in '79.

* * *

CHAPTER XXII.

BROTHER GEORGE.

On the 6th of April, 1864, my brother George was called to go on a mission to Switzerland; and left home on the last of the month, crossing the plains in company with Daniel H. Wells and Brigham Young, Jr., who were appointed to preside over the British mission.

My sister Catherine accompanied her husband and remained in Europe three and a half years.

George arrived in Geneva the 11th of August, and immediately commenced studying the

French language. His companion missionary, W. W. Riter, in a short time was taken ill, and as soon as he was able returned to England, leaving George alone among strangers. On the 20th of November, my brother came down with that most terrible disease, black small pox. The people with whom he stopped were very poor, but kind-hearted, and did the best they could for him. Having only one or two rooms, they put him into a very small room, or closet, under the stairway; he could barely straighten his limbs, and there he remained for over two months, suffering the most intense agony. He was blind and helpless for three weeks; could only speak a few words of the language, and doubtless in his feeble state forgot what he had learned, and knew not how to ask for a drink of water. While in that condition his spirit seemed to leave his body, and the people around him thought him dead. When word reached England of what had befallen George, a good friend and brother by the name of Hill, was immediately sent to his relief, and with good care through the kind providence of our Heavenly

Father, he was restored to health, but disfigured for years.

When he was able to converse, he told his friend where his spirit had traveled on leaving his body. He said, "I thought I was going with a multitude of people to the other world, not realizing at the time that we were without bodies. As we came to a gate or entrance many who were with me passed in, but I was not permitted to do so. And as I wandered along I noticed the crowd scatter and go in different directions. Again I found myself in Salt Lake City, walking up and down the streets, and remember being in front of President Young's house, and seeing many persons that I knew on the sidewalk; but they did not recognize or pay any attention to me. When I came to myself, and found that I was upon this earth, it was made known to me that my spirit had been away, and that when I should die, it would go to that same place and be admitted."

As soon as he had sufficiently recovered, George began studying again, and became quite proficient in both the French and German languages. His mission to Switzerland lasted about three and a half years.

In two weeks after returning from his European mission, George was called, at the October conference, 1867, in connection with others, to go and make a settlement in Nevada. He was advised to get married, and take his wife with him. Accordingly, on the 10th of November, following, he was married to Leonora Horne, daughter of Joseph and M. Isabella Horne. And on the 20th of the same month, with provisions, clothing, and household goods all put into one wagon, drawn by two mules, they started for the Muddy, four hundred and fifty miles south of Salt Lake City. Arriving at their destination on the 16th of December, after a rough and tedious journey. The country looked desolate and forbidding, but the new settlers were not discouraged with the outlook, and commenced to build houses, clear off land, dig ditches, etc., under the most adverse circumstances. The country was noted for its sandy soil, high winds, and in warm weather, an unusual quantity of flies and ants. Therefore the reader can imagine some of the trials endured. Leonora told me afterward what trouble she had in trying to keep the ants out of the victuals, for put them where she would, they were sure to find an entrance.

After a time the mission was broken up. George remained three years and a half, then was honorably released by President Young. He left his house and improvements, without selling, returned to Salt Lake City and commenced anew. One child had been born to them while in the south, a little girl named Lucy Isabella, but none of us ever had the privilege of seeing her, for she died in their southern home on the 16th of January, 1870. The parents could not think of leaving the earthly remains of their loved one in such a far off place, so her body was taken up, and they brought it with them to the city. George got a situation in Zion's Co-operative Mercantile Institution, where he prospered in business until the fall of 1874, when he moved to Paris, Bear Lake. He was bishop of the First Ward of Paris for a few years, also held the office of sheriff of the county.

CHAPTER XXIII.

MISSION TO ARIZONA—A ROMANTIC INCIDENT —FACE TO FACE WITH A BEAR.

EVER since the Latter-day Saints entered the valley of the Great Salt Lake, companies have been sent throughout Utah Territory and into other territories and states to make homes, and form new states, in order that there might be places prepared for the hosts of people that emigrated every year to these valleys.

In the winter of 1875-76 a number of families were selected from different localities to go into Arizona and make settlements. My son Lo'ce was called upon to go, although at that time he had no family, and was working for Z. C. M. I., in Salt Lake City, and receiving a pretty fair salary. He had worked there only a few months and had but little means laid by, yet felt willing to leave all, and accept the mission, when called upon by the proper authority. Brother Lot

Smith, who lived near us, was made President of the mission. The families who went from Farmington, started on the 21st of February, 1876. Their aim in starting so early was to get to their journey's end in time to put in a crop. Arizona was a barren and desolate country, and the emigrants had no success in raising anything the first year, on account of failure in their efforts to get out water from the Colorado River for irrigating purposes; the cause of the failure was so much quicksand in the stream that the dams would not hold. The people passed through many hardships and privations for a few years, yet with the perseverance usually possessed by Latter-day Saints, settlements were made, and some of them are in a flourishing condition at the present time.

After having been gone over two years, Lo'ce came home for a few months, and in August, 1879, was married to Clara Gleason of Farmington, returning to Sunset, Arizona, late in the fall.

At this time the families of Sunset were living in the United Order, all eating in one large dining room built for the purpose; the women taking turns in cooking. The work for the men was divided out to them, some plowing and sowing, others herding, etc. This was supposed to be a trial case, to see what could be accomplished by a few uniting together, and it was a success.

This continued a few years, when at length it was broken up, and their property, which consisted mostly of horses, cattle and sheep, was divided and each family went for itself.

Lo'ce bought a place in Snowflake, Arizona, which has been his home ever since.

While living in Sunset, Lo'ce spent most of his time herding sheep, changing their pasture at times to get better feed. One day while driving them through a wood, he found some money, a notice of which circumstance I will copy from the *Deseret News*:

"A ROMANTIC INCIDENT.

"Andrew Lo'ce Rogers finds over six thousand dollars in gold and returns it to the owners, who were robbed of it six years ago.

"We have been permitted to peruse a letter from Brother Andrew L. Rogers, of Sunset, Apache County, Arizona, to his brother, Orson Rogers, of this city. We make the following interesting extracts:

"'I will explain how I found a mass of gold and what came of it: You remember of yourself finding some money once in an old book, and for your honesty was rewarded with part of it. Mine was a somewhat similar circumstance only on a larger scale.

"'Six years ago Moses Casner and brother had over six thousand dollars stolen from them, all in twenty-dollar gold pieces. The thief in his haste to get away, lost the money off the hind part of his saddle in passing through the timber. He was soon taken prisoner, and in trying to make him tell where the money was, the Casners hung him to a tree until he was nearly dead. In order to save his life the thief told them he had lost the money, but would tell them all he knew about it, and went to help them find it. They piled up rocks where the money was supposed to be lost, and although many men had hunted days for it, it never could be found, so that they gave up all hopes and stopped searching.

"'On the 24th of July, 1882, six years after the loss of the money, as I was following on the track of my sheep, I saw something that I thought consisted of curious looking yellow oak leaves; but a second glance showed it was a pile of gold. I commenced putting it in my pockets but they would not hold it, so I took off my coat tied one sleeve with a string and put it in. I hastily picked up all I could find, and hurried on after my sheep as they were out of sight. Before I got back to camp I had to keep changing from one shoulder to the other. I knew who were the owners of the lost money, as I had heard of the circumstance of the stolen gold. Not being able to leave my sheep, I told Hube Burk to go and tell the Casners, as they lived a number of miles away. They came, and when they saw their lost treasure they could hardly contain themselves for joy. They wanted to know what I charged; I told them nothing. But this would not do for them. Almost any amount would have been given me had I named it, but I did not choose to do this, knowing that I had no more right to their money than if I had never seen it. They said the Lord had a hand in it, for it was not to be found till the right person came along, 'for,' said they, 'if almost any one else had found it we never would have seen it again.' They said it was like a gift to them.

" 'As I had made no charges one of them quickly picked up a pile of money and threw it over to me, and a smaller pile to Brother Burk. Mine was two hundred dollars and Brother Burk's sixty dollars. The Casners then bade us a heartfelt good day and rode for home. The circumstance of my finding the money was a little singular, for in their search for it the Casner's had piled up rocks within ten feet of where it was lying. Thus ended a matter that had caused a good deal of interest and wonder. Twenty dollars of the two hundred I paid for tithing; twenty dollars I keep as I wish to get me a good gun.'

"We may add that one hundred dollars has

been forwarded by this honest, noble-hearted young man to his parents, and the remaining sixty dollars to his wife's mother. There is evidently not only an entire absence of a shade of dishonesty in his composition, but he displays a most refreshing unselfishness.

"Brother Rogers is a native of Farmington, Davis County, is the son of Thomas and Aurelia Rogers. The late Orson Spencer was his grandfather, and he is cousin to Mr. Spencer Clawson of this city. He was born and reared in the Church."

The circumstance of his brother Orson finding a sum of money, alluded to in the letter, occurred in Z. C. M. I. When he handed it over to General Eldredge, who was Superintendent at the time, that gentleman gave him some of it.

———

There is another incident in Lo'ce's life which I think is worthy of note, and might be called

FACE TO FACE WITH A BEAR.

The following is given in his own words:

"On a pleasant afternoon in the latter part of

August, the sheep were feeding quietly on the south slope of the Dairy Mountain, Yavapai County, Arizona, when suddenly I saw them rushing like a mighty avalanche, pell mell, down the mountain, directly toward me. I looked to see the cause of their great alarm, and what was my surprise to see a huge bear right at their heels.

"I had nothing with me but a little stick and a jack knife, but felt determined to save the sheep if possible. So, hastily picking up a few stones, I ran towards the bear, saying as I went, 'stop, you son of a gun, let those sheep alone, or I'll kill you.'

"The bear stopped in his mad chase, set back upon his haunches and looked at me. I also had stopped, the sheep having passed me, and there we stood face to face within a short distance of each other.

"The thought of danger had not at first entered my mind, as I was thinking only of the safety of the sheep, but as I neared the bear, a feeling of fear came over me, and I gave a quick side glance, for a suitable tree to climb, in case of necessity. After looking at each other a few moments the bear cast his eyes on the sheep who were fast disappearing down the slope, then got down on all fours and walked slowly away in the opposite direction.

"The fact that I had mere nothing to defend myself with, was almost laughable, but the saying came to my mind, that 'the true shepherd would die for his sheep.''

CHILDREN OF ORSON AND CATHARINE CURTIS SPENCER.

Catharine Curtis, born October 6th, 1831; died December 24th, 1833.
Ellen Curtis, born November 21, 1832; died August 25, 1896.
Aurelia Read, born October 4, 1834.
Catharine Read, born October 2, 1836.
Howard Orson, born June 16, 1838.
George Boardman, born February 21, 1840.
Lucy Curtis, born October 9, 1842; died December 29, 1867.
Chloe, born July 26, 1844; died September 6, 1845.

CHILDREN OF ORSON AND MARTHA KNIGHT SPENCER.

Martha Emma, born January 30, 1848.

Albert James, born June 24, 1850.

William Collinson, born December 10, 1851; died November 12, 1853.

June Knight, born June 28, 1854.

DAUGHTER OF ORSON AND JANE DAVIS SPENCER.

Luna, born December 6, 1852.

Orson Spencer was the father of thirteen children. His grandchildren, up to 1897 number ninety-two, and great grandchildren, about one hundred and twenty-five.

PART SECOND.

CHAPTER I.

HISTORY OF PRIMARY WORK—LETTER FROM E. R. SNOW.

IN writing this sketch of the commencement of our Primaries, it is my desire, and shall be my aim to present it in a way that shall be plain to the understanding of all.

In August, 1878, I was called upon to preside over a Primary Association in Farmington. I was always an earnest thinker, and naturally of a religious turn of mind. And for some time previous to the organization of the children, I had reflected seriously upon the necessity of more strict discipline for our little boys.

Many of them were allowed to be out late at night; and certainly some of the larger ones well deserved the undesirable name of "hoodlum." It may seem strange that in a community calling themselves Latter-day Saints, children should be allowed to indulge in anything approaching to rowdyism. But it must be remembered that the age in which we live is one that tends to carelessness in the extreme, not only in regard to religion, but also morality. And not only this, but in many intances our people have been driven about and persecuted on every hand, until it has seemed to be all they could do to make a living for their children; and an apology might almost be made for negligence in training them up. Yet why should anything be allowed to come before the most sacred duty of parentage, that of looking after the spiritual welfare of the children? was the question which burdened my mind.

Our Bishop must have been similarly impressed, for a meeting of the mothers of our little ones was called by him, at which much good advice and counsel was given.

The subject of training children was thoroughly discussed and the responsibility of guiding their young minds was thrown almost entirely upon the mothers. I had children of my own, and was just as anxious as a mother could be to have them brought up properly. But what was to be done? It needed the united effort of the parents, and, as is often the case in a community, some of them were careless. A fire seemed to burn within me, and I had a desire at one time to go to the Young Men's Mutual Improvement Association meeting and talk to them; but I did not yield to the impulse, thinking too much, perhaps, of what people might say. The query then arose in my mind could there not be an organization for little boys wherein they could be taught everything good, and how to behave. This was in March; a few weeks later Sister Eliza R. Snow Smith and Sister Emmeline B. Wells, from Salt Lake City, came to Farmington to attend a Relief Society Conference.

After meeting was over, and when on their way to the depot, these sisters in company with Sisters Mary S. Clark, Nancy Clark, and Lorinda Robinson, stopped at my home for a short call. The topic of our conversation was the young people, and the rough, careless ways many of the young men and boys had at the time. I asked the question, "What will our girls do for good husbands, if this state of things continues?" Sister Eliza seemed deeply impressed with the question; and then I asked.

"Could there not be an organization for little boys, and have them trained to make better men?"

She was silent a few moments, then said there might be such a thing and that she would speak to the First Presidency about it.

The death of President Brigham Young occurred on the 29th of August, 1877: and at the time of the beginning of the Primaries, President John Taylor with his quorum of the Twelve Apostles, presided over the Church.

Sister Eliza consulted with Apostle John Taylor and others of the Twelve, concerning this new move, and it was approved of by them. She accordingly wrote a lettter to Bishop Hess and explained the matter to him. He visited me soon after receiving her letter, and when we had talked awhile on the subject, he asked me if I would be willing to preside over an organization of the children. I felt willing, but very incompetent. From that time my mind was busy thinking how it was to be managed.

Up to this period the girls had not been mentioned; but my mind was that the meeting would not be complete without them; for as singing was necessary, it needed the voices of little girls as well as boys to make it sound as well as it should. After some consideration, a letter was sent to Sister Eliza asking her opinion in regard to the little girls taking part.

The following letter was received in answer to mine.

"SALT LAKE CITY, AUG. 4, 1878.
"My dear sister Rogers: The spirit and contents of your letter pleased me much. I feel assured that the inspiration of heaven is directing you, and that a great and very important movement is being inaugurated for the future of Zion.

"Your letter was waiting my return from Provo Valley on Thursday evening—yesterday (Sat.) I read it in our general meeting in the Fourteenth Ward Assembly Rooms.

"Soon after my return from Farmington I proposed to Sister Mary J. Thompson to move forward in the Sixteenth Ward and establish a president, requesting her to suggest a whole souled brother who would enter into the spirit of the work; and last evening with her, I called on Brother Perkins, whose feelings were fully enlisted as soon as we informed him of the object in question. He is in daily employment during the week, and although a constant attendant at Sabbath service is willing to devote the afternoon to the benefit of the children, and for the time being deprive himself the enjoyment of the Sacrament. The importance of the movement, and its great necessity is fully acknowledged by all with whom I have conversed on the subject.

"President John Taylor fully approbates it, and Joseph F. Smith thinks we might better afford what expense might be incurred in furnishing uniform, musical instruments etc, for the cultivation of the children in Zion, than what we are expending in converting people abroad where elders spend years in converting a very few.

"We think that at present, it will be wisdom to not admit any under six years of ago, except in some special instances. You are right—we must have the girls as well as the boys—they must be trained together.

"I think your mind will be directed to a brother who will unite with you in establishing this movement. Brother Perkins thinks that plenty of assistance will be forthcoming as the work progresses. The angels and all holy beings, especially the leaders of Israel on the other side the veil will be deeply interested.

"I wish to see and converse with you, but cannot make it convenient at present. Tomorrow is election—on the 6th, if the Lord wills I shall go to Mendon—attend the sisters' Quarterly Conference in Ogden on the 15th and 16th—go to West Porterville on the 17th and return home sometime about the 20th. If I can so arrange will see you on my return.

"That God will continue to inspire you in the establishment and development of this great movement, is the earnest prayer of

"Your sister and fellow laborer,

"E. R. Snow."

Sister Eliza in company with Sister M. Isabella Horne visited me soon after. Sister Snow suggested that the organization be called "Primary."

✣ ✣ ✣

CHAPTER II.

PRIMARY WORK CONTINUED.

While thinking over what was to be done for the best good of the children, I seemed to be carried away in the spirit, or at least I experienced a feeling of untold happiness which lasted three days and nights. During that time nothing could worry or irritate me; if my little ones were fretful, or the work went wrong, I had patience, could control in kindness, and manage my household affairs easily. This was a testimony to me that what was being done was from God.

On Sunday, August 11th, 1878, at a public meeting, I was set apart by Bishop John W.

Hess and his Counselors Arthur Stayner and Jacob Miller, to preside over a Primary Association in Farmington, with Mrs. Louisa Haight and Mrs. Helen M. Miller as my counselors. Soon after Mrs. Rhoda H. Richards was chosen Secretary and Miss Clara A. Leonard, Treasurer.

Sister Richard's health being very poor her daughter, Sarah E., assisted her, and in a short time took her place as Secretary. Bishop Hess, who was zealous in every good cause, suggested that myself and counselors visit the ward and get the names of all the children of a suitable age, and see if the parents were willing for them to attend meeting. This we did, visiting every house, taking the name and age of each child to the number of two hundred and twenty-four. I have the record now and prize it very much. We were counseled to find some good brother to assist us in our labors at first, to insure success, as the move was a new one. Brother Mads Christenson was selected, and proved to be a good help indeed. He made a book-case to put our books in, also a table, giving us his labor free of charge.

It has been stated that just previous to the organization I enjoyed a feeling of happiness such as I had never known before. One thing that seemed strange to me, was, that after the organization I was nearly overcome by the opposite power, and was sunken, as it were, into the very depths of misery; I felt my unworthiness so keenly that I could scarcely attend to my duties; and went to my meetings weeping by the way, being humbled to the very earth; so much so, that whatever any one said afterward in my praise, did not make me feel exalted, or lifted up in my own mind. I had been made to feel my entire dependence on God the Eternal Father.

The children were called together for the first time on the 25th of August, 1878, the object of the meeting was explained to them, and another one appointed, which was duly held on the 7th of September. And from that time on, our meetings were held every Saturday at 2 p. m. in the meeting house. (September 7, is a memorable day with many of our sisters in Zion, as the birthday of "Aunt Prescendia Kimball."

When the children came to understand the motives which prompted the calling of their little meetings, they seemed elated with what was being done for them. We asked them if they would try to be punctual and assist us by keeping good order; they were willing to try to do their best. My assistants and myself took turns in presiding over the meetings.

It would be impossible for one who had never experienced anything of the kind, to imagine our feelings as we stood before an audience of children who had come there to receive instructions from us. We were very weak indeed, but felt to lean upon the Lord in all humility.

At first the children were very timid about singing; Brother Joseph E. Robinson came in a few times and assisted in starting them. Finally their voices rang out sweet and clear, and in some cases much talent was displayed.

Aside from the instructions we gave, there were program and testimony meetings.

Obedience, faith in God, prayer, punctuality and good manners were subjects oft repeated; and we always endeavored to impress the children with the fact that home is the place to begin to practice all good things. Sometimes we would ask them how many would like to try for one week, and see how much they could do for father and mother without grumbling, and not quarrel with their brothers and sisters. A good many would try; and we heard from several of the mothers afterwards, who had noticed quite a change for the better in their children. Among other things which we taught, were that the Lord sees our actions, and knows everything we do in secret; and that when sick we can be healed if we have faith enough, without having to call in a doctor.

We would ask the children before the opening prayer of the meeting, if they knew of any one who was ill and needed our special prayers, if so aprayer was offered up to the Lord in their behalf; and in a number of instances the sick were helped immediately, which strengthened the faith of the little ones. This taught them to think of the sufferings of others, and to cultivate a desire to comfort and bless everyone. The principle of honesty was a leading feature in the instructions given; the children were encouraged in this, by having impressed upon their minds that when they found anything, they were to seek diligently to restore it to the owner. To assist them in this they were told that they might bring articles found to their meetings, and have them advertized.

It was very gratifying and sometimes amusing to see how readily the little ones took hold of this suggestion, and how earnest they were in working it out. Frequently articles were brought to us and the owners found right there at the meeting. In cases where the owner could not be found, after every effort had been made that could be, the finder of an article was allowed to keep it.

At one time a dollar green-back was picked up on the side walk, by a little girl on her way to meeting; it was thoroughly advertised, but the owner was never discovered. The little girl felt very rich and happy, and well paid for her honesty, when the money became lawfully her own.

CHAPTER III.

QUARTERLY MEETINGS—PLANTING BEANS.

Every three months a quarterly meeting was held, and a special program arranged for the occasion. The parents were invited, and sometimes we had visitors from Salt Lake City. Sister Eliza came to our first quarterly meeting, and spoke highly of the progress we were making.

At these meetings, the whole association would generally take part in the exercises. The smaller children were seated on the front benches, the rest according to size all the way through. At the proper time the smallest would rise up and, perhaps, recite a verse or two in concert, then sit down and the next bench full take their turn in answering Bible questions. Another class would sing a song; another would repeat sentiments or verses, one at a time, and so on. Our larger boys and girls assisted us in training these classes, which work they enjoyed very much, and it also lightened our labors.

The Word of Wisdom, Section 89 of the Doctrine and Covenants, was talked upon in one of our quarterly meetings, and explained as being the word of God to us; the children were asked how many would try to observe it for the next three months.

At the end of the term, forty-three names were recorded as having kept the Word of Wisdom for that length of time; and sixty-five more names were added at the end of the second quarter. In later years we have heard some of these children, who have since grown to manhood and womanhood, testify that they have never tasted tea or coffee, neither used tobacco or drank liquor of any kind, since that time.

The next spring we rented a town lot and the Primary Association, with Brother Christensen at the head, planted beans and pop-corn. The plowing and watering of the lot were done by our husbands and sons. The lot was divided into twelve sections, and twenty-four of our largest boys and girls took their portion of ground to cultivate. When the beans and corn came out of the ground they were expected to keep them weeded and tended to, until ripe; then harvest them, and after the tithing was paid, they were to be put into the Primary treasury for safe keeping. We have some of those beans now; they are yellow with age, but perfectly sound. Pop corn balls were made out of the corn thus provided, for the children's party the next Christmas. Our motive in raising beans was to have beans to go with the Relief Society wheat, in the time of famine which is to come.

At our first annual meeting, sixteen yards of carpet had been made by the members of the Association; the girls sewing the rags, and the boys donating five cents each, to buy the warp and pay for the weaving. This carpet was placed on exhibition by hanging it over the stand in the meeting house, so that the children could have a good view of it, and was afterwards donated to help in building the Salt Lake Temple. For a number of years in succession, a carpet was made by the Association for the same purpose.

At this, our first annual meeting, a concert was held, and a happy lot of children took part therein; it was free for every body, and many of the parents came in and listened to the songs, recitations and dialogues of the little folks. This is a history in brief of the first year's labor in the Primary.

✤ ✤ ✤

CHAPTER IV.

SISTER ELIZA'S WORK IN ORGANIZING—LOUIE B. FELT'S CALLING.

THE interest manifested by Sister Eliza R. Snow at the beginning of the Primary work never slackened. She was truly a woman of God, and may her name ever be remembered and cherished by the children of the Latter-day Saints. It was through her energy and labor that Primaries were organized throughout the Territory of Utah. The Lord had not given her children of her own, but her loving care was extended to all the dear children everywhere. She went from place to place, in company with Sister Zina D. H. Young and others, organizing with the assistance of the Bishops until nearly every settlement had a Primary Association. It was Sister Eliza who arranged the selections for the Primary hymn-book, also the First and Second Speakers, and Bible Questions and Answers. She engaged Mrs. Doctor Ferguson to arrange the music for the songs, which was called the Tune Book.

In April, 1879, my sister, Ellen Clawson, was chosen to preside over a Primary in the Twelfth Ward, Salt Lake City. While attending their first annual meeting, Sister Eliza, being one of the visitors, came to me and said it was thought best to have some one appointed to preside over all the Primary Associations in the Territory. She suggested that the person should reside in Salt Lake City, as that was the center; and asked me whom I would propose to fill the office.

I said I could not tell on so short notice, but would reflect a few moments. After doing so the name of Sister Louie B. Felt came to my mind. As soon as I told Sister Eliza, she said that was her choice, and also Sister Clawson's. This satisfied me that Sister Felt was the one to hold that important office.

She was President of the Primary Association in the Eleventh Ward, Salt Lake City, which was the second one organized, following close upon ours in Farmington; and she had been a very interested visitor at one of our early quarterly meetings. From the first time I ever met Sister Felt, an unusually warm feeling of sympathetic friendship seemed to draw me towards her.

When she was chosen to preside over all the Primary Associations, some persons thought it was my place to hold that position. But I wish to say here, that I never had a moment's jealousy over anyone holding office; for no person will ever take my honors from me; I shall have all that I deserve.

On the 19th of June, 1880, Sister Louie B. Felt was set apart to fill the responsible position of presiding over our Primary Associations in all the world: At the same meeting my sister Ellen Clawson was chosen and set apart to preside over the Primary Associations of Salt Lake Stake. My calling was to preside over those in the Davis Stake; having been duly appointed on the 16th of July, 1880; with Sisters Julia Hess and Lucy A. Clark for my counselors, Miss Sarah E. Richards, secretary, and Sister Anna M. Wilcox, treasurer.

※ ※ ※

CHAPTER V.

PRIMARY FAIRS—MARTIAL MUSIC.

The children's Fairs commenced in 1880. Mrs. Ann Dustin, President of East Bountiful Primary, being the originator of the idea, the first fair was held in that settlement. Much credit was due both the officers and the little folks for their perseverance in making so many useful and ornamental articles. Our first Primary fair in Farmington opened in

June, a few days later than the one in East Bountiful.

For our Fairs the boys contributed things which they had made; hay-racks, ladders, rakes, wheelbarrows, tables,c upboards, chairs, clothes-racks, bee-hives, and numerous other articles. They also brought samples of grain, vegetables and fruit which they had helped to raise. Fine specimens of drawing, painting and penmanship were presented both by boys and girls; and the latter gave freely of their handiwork, in sewing, knitting, straw-braiding, darning, mending, patch-work, fancy-work, bread-making and pastry; they also brought fresh fruit put up in bottles, and a variety of dried fruit. Our Farmington Primary, and also other Associations in Davis County, donated of their substance to the Deseret Hospital. Following is a sample of the receipts given.

SALT LAKE CITY, September, 1888.

Received of Farmington Primary Association, 32 bottles of fruit, 2 bottles of pickles, also 3 two quart bottles of fruit, and 20 ears of popcorn as a donation to the Deseret Hospital.

Romania B. Pratt, Res. Physician.

We do not mention having donated these things with the desire to have our good deeds "proclaimed upon the house tops," but to show up a principle.

If there are no temples being built at the present time, nor hospitals that we wish to assist, the poor we have always with us, and we can make a specialty of our coming fairs, in helping those who are not so well off as ourselves. To show that Sister Eliza Snow Smith approved of holding fairs I will copy from one of her letters.

Salt Lake City, Oct. 15, 1881.

"Mrs. A. S. Rogers,

"Beloved Sister:—At last I have taken my pen, determined to write you, which I have wished to do, and should have done long since. You know how it is without my telling; with the thousand and one things to do, what can be deferred is most sure to be.

"I congratulate you and all other sisters who energetically promoted or encouraged the movement of Primary Fairs. I am thankful that the Stake Fair in this City was kept open till after my return from Sanpete. I had anticipated much, but it far exceeded my anticipations.

"I think great good will result from the children's Fairs, not only in developing the inventive powers of the childen; but in occupying their minds usefully and preventing them running into folly. I hope you will find my little book of Questions and Answers, to be an assistant to the officers of the Primary Associations. Praying that you and all the dear sisters may have health and strength equal to your arduous labors and noble desires,

"I am your loving sister,
"E. R. S. S."

There is danger of dishonesty being thoughtlessly encouraged in these fairs if we do not guard against it. Children are apt to be quite elated over making things to place on exhibition, and many times take the entire credit of doing what some one else has helped them to do. It is not expected that our boys and girls can make all such articles as those previously mentioned without the assistance or instruction of father, mother, or others. Then why not have the truth stated on the label? For instance, "Hay-rack made by John Smith, assisted by his father." After awhile he will be able to do the work alone or with a little showing; then, and not till then, should he take the honor of having done the work by himself.

In January, 1882, a Primary Martial Band was organized in Farmington. The instruments used were flutes, piccolos, a triangle, and three drums. Mr. Hedger from Salt Lake City, was the teacher; he was proficient and thorough, and although it was their first lessons in music, with many of the boys, yet they learned fast, and in two months could play several tunes. Then was the time for serenading the town of Farmington. A happy lot of boys (some of them quite small) with Brother James Loynd for their captain, marched through the streets making sweet music; stopping occasionally at some of the houses, where they were treated to cakes and lemonade, or candy and nuts. Quite a little money was also received from the people, which was used to help pay for their music lessons. There have been other Primary bands organized in our County, and we anticipate having more of them: for we wish to encourage in our children a love for music, also a love for all things beautiful, which includes the cultivation of flowers. We believe that the Lord is pleased with lovely homes, and when they are made beautiful with the workmanship of our own hands, it is gratifying to behold or to reflect upon them.

CHAPTER VI.

DISCOURAGEMENT.—HAPPY RESULT.

For the benefit of those who are engaged in teaching children, I will relate an incident which gave me quite an experience.

It was in the fall of 1885. I had presided over the Primary Association of Farmington for seven years, and with all my anxiety and labor to get the boys to attend meeting, had, in a measure, failed. This tried me very much, for these Associations were instituted for the good of the little boys especially, and when but few came to meeting, and it seemed hard to interest them, at times I was quite discouraged. I felt to blame the parents, particularly the fathers, and thought if they were more interested their boys could be spared from work, and encouraged to attend their meetings. With these feelings I made up my mind not to worry any more, but leave them in the hands of the Lord, and when He saw fit to wake the people up things might be different.

While in this state of mind, word was sent to me from Salt Lake City, to see if I could go to Utah County and visit the children's Association. The invitation was accepted, and in company with Mrs. Sarah M. Kimball and Mrs. Elmina S. Taylor, I started south on the 19th of October, 1885. Sisters Kimball and Taylor were going in the interest of the Relief, and Young Ladies' Societies.

At a young people's meeting in Payson, on the 21st of October, in the course of the evening, I was called upon to speak; and although shrinking within myself at the thought of facing so many people, I arose and said a few words, in which I expressed a desire to some day be able to speak my thoughts; but knew this could not be, without making an effort to help myself. When I said these words, it came to my mind that Oliver Cowdery at one time when called upon to translate, had an idea that the Lord would dictate, and he would have nothing else to do but write it down. The Lord told him by revelation, this was not what He wanted; He expected Oliver to think for himself, and if what came into his mind was pleasing to the Lord, his bosom would burn within him, and he would feel that it was right; and if it were not right, he would have a stupor of thought, that would cause him to forget all that was wrong; so I mentioned this to the congregation.

It was the feeling I had afterwards that made it so important to me; for in reflecting upon what had been said at the meeting, I felt convinced that what had been given me to say about Oliver Cowdery was for my own particular benefit, and I saw the course marked out for me to pursue in regard to Primaries. I had felt to cease my exertions to get the boys out to meeting thinking the Lord would manage it for me, and most assuredly He did in His own way.

This was a lesson; and it was made plain to me that we must think for ourselves, and if we fail in one thing, try another. I felt determined to be more diligent in my duties ever after, and upon returning home went to work with a will and had good success with the Primary children. I arranged them in classes according to their size, placing a larger boy or girl, at the end of each bench as monitors, letting these keep the roll of their classes in little note books given them for the purpose. These registers were afterwards recorded by the head secretary.

With all the difficulties encountered, I have indeed had joy in my Primary labors; and feel that it was this work that President Heber C. Kimball saw when conversing with me at the door of the Photograph Gallery.

His cautioning me not to tell everything I knew was timely, for speaking too freely when in conversation with others, was one of my weaknesses; and I profited by the counsel given.

CHAPTER VII.

CO-LABORERS—PLEASANT SURPRISES.

While presiding over the Farmington Primary Association, I had occasion to have two more counselors other than those before mentioned. Sister Louisa Haight who had been a faithful help to me for a number of years, was obliged to move north, her husband, Horton D. Haight, having been called to preside over a branch in Oakley, Idaho.

Soon after, Sister Miller was appointed to take Sister Haight's place, as First Counselor, and Miss Sarah E. Richards was chosen for my Second Counselor. Up to this time, she held the office of Secretary, keeping the books in good order. She was afterward married to Loren Robinson, and in a few years they also moved to Oakley. Miss Anna Clark was the next one selected as a counselor, and held the position for a short time, giving good satisfaction.

Sister Helen M. Miller was ever by my side in laboring with the children, until I was released from Primary duties in the Ward, (my duties in the Stake being all that I could well attend to.) This occurred in August, 1887, at which time Sister Wealthy Clark took my place as President over the Primary Association in Farmington. She held the office one year, when, on account of poor health and home cares, she was released. Sister Jane Smith was the next President, which office she held four years.

On the 11th of August, 1892, Miss Annette Abbott was voted in as President, with Miss Mary Millard, and Mrs. Minerva Knowlton as her counselors. In 1896, Miss Mary Millard took the Presidency. I wish to thank the Presidents of the Associations under my jurisdiction, with their counselors, the secretaries, treasurers, and all the members, for their confidence in me. They have expressed their love for me in different ways. The first public demonstration of the kind was a surprise by our own Primary children in Farmington. The members donated the means, and Sister Helen

M. Burns pieced the outside to a handsome quilt, which with the lining, was presented to me one Saturday afternoon at our Primary meeting. I had not language to express my feelings at the time, but wish to make a memorandum of the event in my history, so if any who were at the meeting that day should ever read this book, the incident will come back, fresh to their minds.

On another occasion, September 26th, 1885, at a Primary Conference held in Farmington, the children of our Association presented me with a nice plush covered album; also presented Sister Helen Miller with a likeness of President John Taylor, encased in a plush frame. Sister Miller at that time was my only counselor.

At the time of the presentation I remember Mabel Walker handing me a note which should have been read, but in my surprise, and confusion it was omitted, therefore to make amends I insert it here to be read now.

NOTE FROM THE MEMBERS OF THE PRIMARY.

"SISTER ROGERS AND SISTER MILLER:

"The children of your Association, whom you both for so long a time have instructed, wish to show their appreciation and gratitude for your services. We have thrown our little mites together and purchased for you, Sister Rogers, this Album, and for you, Sister Miller, this picture, and wish you to accept them as a token of our esteem and love."

There are other instances of the kind which I wish to mention, as it is all that I can do to show my appreciation of the honors conferred.

The first was under the management of the Presidency of the East Bountiful Primary Association; namely, Ann Dustin, President; Mary Evans, Sarah Eastrope, Margaretta Call, Counselors; in connection with the following names from East Bountiful, Olive Sessions Corbridge, and baby, Lucina Sessions, Jr., Byrena Dustin, and Brother Day, teamster. Also Ortentia Leonard, Helen M. Miller, Sarah E. Richards, Julia Hess, Lucy A. Clark, and twin girls three weeks old, Mary S. Clark, and Lizzie Cotterell, from Farmington gave me a surprise by coming to my house October 17th, 1881, bringing their baskets full of good things to eat. Little did I think what was coming, when Sister Ortentia Leonard, President of the Relief Society, came in that morning to spend a few hours with me, as she said. A short time after, a team drove up to the door, and I wondered how it was that the sisters from Bountiful should happen to come on that day; but when my neighbors came also, I began to see through the mystery.

We did indeed have a pleasant interview, during which time I was presented with a loving Testimonial in fancy penmanship, nicely framed, from the Presidency of the East Bountiful Association. Also some dishes, a lovely glass set, and other things from the sisters of Farmington. Brother Ezra T. Clark, Brother Day and my husband, joined us in the enjoyment of the luxuries of the baskets.

Another time, on the 28th of December, 1888, I was just recovering from a severe spell of sickness, which had lasted seven weeks, and was not able to sit up all day; had lain down to rest when the door opened and Sister Maria Hatch, (President of the South Bountiful Primary) came in; this surprised me some; but soon after as other dear faces kept making their appearance, one after another, until the room was nearly full, I learned that the Primary Officers of Davis Stake had met here, as they said, to show their appreciation of my labors in the past. I remember how heavenly the countenances of the sisters looked as they came in at the door; it was indeed like the visit of angels come to rest and soothe my wearied body and mind. Sister Julia Hess, my first counselor, was unanimously chosen to take charge of the exercises, to which she responded in her original, happy way with brief but pointed remarks. She thought it would be well to open the meeting with singing and prayer. Sister Wealthy Clark was nominated to take minutes of the proceedings. After which, all stood up and sang "Love at home," accompanied on the organ by Miss Viola Chase, (for through the management of Miss Kate Chase, an organ had been brought to the house, we did not own one.) Prayer was offered by Elder Thomas Rogers. Singing, "O, My Father, Thou That Dwellest."

Sister Hess then made a few remarks, followed by Counselor Lucy A. Clark, who recited an original poem on friendship.

The other sisters present also expressed their love and esteem for me in a few appropriate words, hoping that I would soon be restored to health.

The speakers were Sisters Anna Rockwood, Kate Chase, (who also read letters from some of the Presidents not present, expressing their regrets at not being able to come,) Elizabeth Ford, Jane Smith, Wealthy Clark, Maggie Grant, Lucy Muir, Maria Hatch, Jane Pack, Eveline Benson, Mamie Lamb Robinson, Mamie Stevenson, and Monica Secrist. During the meeting I sat up in bed and thanked the Sisters in my feeble way for their visit. Saying that words could not express my gratitude, and although some of the Presidents were absent, I thought of them, and they all seemed very dear to me; and I cherished their love and good wishes more than gold or silver. Made other remarks, then closed by asking the blessing of God upon all.

Between the speeches the hymn, "Nay Speak No Ill," had been sung.

I was then presented with a beautiful plush wrap, which was indeed a surprise, and was received with gratitude. "The Spirit of God Like a Fire is Burning," was sung.

The tables were then spread, and about twenty-five persons sat down to a bounteous repast. The President of the Stake, William R. Smith, his First Counselor, John W. Hess, Bishop Secrist and others, had been invited in at the close of the Priesthood meeting. After supper, the brethren administered to me, when the company dispersed.

It was during this illness that I was strongly impressed to write a sketch of my life. These thoughts had come to my mind at different times previously, but I had banished them, not feeling capable to undertake such a task. Now it could not be put off; something seemed to urge me on, and I resolved if my life were spared, to commence writing immediately, or so soon as I was able.

In two weeks after coming down with this illness, I was much better, so much so that I could dress myself and sit up in my rocking chair. On this day, the 28th of November, 1888, I wrote the first page of my book. The same evening something I ate for supper disagreed with me; a relapse ensued, and for five weeks I kept my room. The writing of my book was thus delayed; nevertheless it had been commenced, and was continued at intervals, as circumstances would permit.

CHAPTER VIII.

EXTRACTS FROM MY JOURNAL.

IN the Summer of 1882, I received a letter from my brother-in-law, Brigham Young. Enclosed was an order on Cutler's Store; a handsome present, sent by request of sister Catherine, which was duly appreciated. Cutler's Store in Salt Lake City, is a place where they keep home made goods; that is, cloth and other articles made in Utah; and I thus had the privilege of testing the qualities of some of those fabrics.

In the fall of 1882, by invitation of my sister Ellen, and through the courtesy of her husband, H. B. Clawson, I visited the Temple at St. George in the southern part of Utah, in company with President John Taylor and others. While there, met my brother Howard from Orderville, who had come for the purpose of assisting in doing work for our dead kindred.

The Temple is a grand structure, built of

white granite. I enjoyed the sight very much, especially in going upon the roof and taking a view of the surrounding country.

On our way to St. George, while stopping at Scipio, Millard Co., we stayed over night with an elderly couple by the name of Wasden, who were very nice people indeed. In the course of the evening, Sister Wasden happened to mention the name of Orson Spencer; we asked her if she was acquainted with him, and told her we were his daughters. Her surprise was great; she then related an incident which was full of interest to us. Said while living in Cincinnati, Ohio, she had sickness among her children, and one of them died; they were at that time in poor circumstances, and had no means to buy a coffin to bury their dead. It was then that Orson Spencer came to their relief; (this happened when my father was on his last mission,) he bought a coffin, and helped them to some little comforts besides. When Brother and Sister Wasden asked how they could repay him for his kindnes, he said "I want nothing, only if you should be prospered and go to the Valley of the Great Salt Lake, and ever meet any of my children, and can do them a favor, that will be pay enough." We thought it providential, our being led to their house.

July 20th, 1883, I went to Kaysville to attend a Relief Society Conference. After meeting was out, a few of the sisters, namely, Eliza R. Snow Smith, Zina D. Young, Mary S. Clark, Nancy Clark, Mary Richards, Ada Williams, Anna Clark and myself, went with Sister Layton, President of the Relief Society in Kaysville, to her home; where we had a good visit in talking over the things of the Kingdom.

I had often wondered whether Jesus could know anything about the pains of women. Sister Eliza happened to say at that time, that God in order to be God, must know the suffering of woman as well as man. Why had I not thought of this before? It opened up a new train of thought. Was not the Creator greater than the creature! In making machinery, does not the machinist understand every minutiæ of his work? Then does not God understand our organization, and could He not heal a wound, or mend a broken limb, as well as a machinist could repair anything he had made? The Lord instructs us in the Doctrine and Covenants, and tells us what to do for our sick. All that is wanting is faith sufficient. If we have faith, we will keep the commandments of God, and observe the laws of health and life; and by keeping His commandments, our faith is always strengthened.

November 12th, 1884, received a picture, "The representative women of Deseret." Presented by Brother Frank and Sister Minerva Knowlton.

November 24th, my son Curtis was accidentally shot by some boys who were shooting off a small cannon. He received six duck shot in his head and body, but was not permanently hurt.

I saw Wilford Stevenson and Don Walker lead Curty in at the gate, and noticed their pale faces. They had washed the blood off Curty's face, and pulled his hat over his forehead, so I could not see the wound, for Curty had told them it would scare me so to see the blood. Brave, thoughtful little boys! They had used this precaution, thinking if they did not, it might give me a shock, and make me sick. This was a warning to them, for some of the boys had been in the habit of playing with fire-arms, against their parents wish, and more serious harm might have come of it.

During the year of '85, and until '87, I taught the Buddington dress cutting with good success. But gave up the business as I found it interfered with my Primary duties.

※ ※ ※

CHAPTER IX.

VISITS TO SUMMIT COUNTY, UTAH, AND TO CASSIA COUNTY, IDAHO.

I WENT to Kamas, Summit County, in September '87, with Sister Zina D. H. Young, to attend the conference of the Relief Society and the Young Ladies' and Primary Associations.

I was invited through the kindness of Sister Louisa Roundy, an old friend of mine, who presided over the Primaries in that Stake.

We left Salt Lake City on the 28th; went as far as Wanship by train, where we took dinner at the house of Bishop E. R. Young, his wife kindly making us welcome. Bishop Samuel Atwood of Kamas, met us at Wanship, and after a ride of fifteen miles, we arrived at his house, where for the first time I saw his wife and family, who spared no pains to make us comfortable. On Thursday, September 30th, attended the Relief Society Conference in a hall built for the recreation of the young people.

President Cluff, Bishop Atwood and other brethren met with us. On Friday the Young Ladies held their Conference. In the evening, went home with Sister John Pack, where we stayed all night.

Saturday, the children had their meeting, which was very interesting; there were quite a number of the parents in attendance. Saturday night, went home with Sister Roundy, who lived in Peoa, about eight miles from Kamas.

Had a good visit, in talking over old times, for we were girls together, and companions. Sister Zina went a mile or two farther on to stay with Sister Gibbons, a friend of hers. Held meetings on Sunday afternoon and evening. Stayed with Sister Gibbons all night. Early on Monday morning, October 3rd, Brother Gibbons took us in his carriage to Wanship, where we took train for home, having spent a most enjoyable time, never to be forgotten.

In September, 1891, I took a trip to Oakley, Idaho, by invitation of Sisters Louisa Haight, and Sarah E. Robinson, my former counselors in the Primary. They wished me to visit Oakley, in company with Sister Zina D. H. Young and Sister Jane S. Richards, to attend the Conferences of the Relief Society and young people, which were to commence on the 19th of September. Accordingly on the evening of the 15th, I went as far as Ogden and stopped over night at the house of Apostle Franklin D. Richards, who had arranged to go with us to Oakley, to visit his daughter, Mrs. Sarah E. Robinson. The next evening Elder F. D. Richards and wife, Sister Young and myself started North, taking the train as far as Kelton Station, ninety miles from Ogden. We arrived at Kelton about ten o'clock at night. Here we met Brother Horton D. Haight, (President of Cassia Stake,) who had come seventy-five miles in a carriage to meet us. At Kelton I met an old acquaintance by the name of Emma Palmer Manfull, whom I was pleased to see; she had been one of my first Primary girls. The next day we traveled forty-five miles to Almo, staying all night with the family of Bishop Thomas King, who took particular pains to make us comfortable. In the evening some of the brethren and sisters came in and we held a very interesting meeting.

On leaving Almo, President Haight called our attention to a place where some emigrants had been murdered by the Indians before the country was settled, with the exception of a ranch or two.

We saw where they had piled up the dirt as a defense, and where they no doubt had struggled and fought for dear life. Only two or three persons had escaped to tell the story, and they nearly perished before being picked up by some of the ranch men. Farther on we passed through what is called the City of Rocks, situated in the Goose Creek range of mountains. It was indeed a grand sight, so many rocks in such curious shapes. In imagination, one could see the ruins of palaces, and houses of all kinds down to the Indian wickeup. On one rock we saw the form of a woman sitting down; farther on, a man standing; also animals of different kinds, at another place, what resembled two girls standing together, and in the distance a cemetery with shrubs and small trees interspersed among the tombs. The huge rocks that stood out in open relief, might have been likened to business houses, or hotels in a city. I have heard of people going to Italy or Switzerland to take a view of the beautiful scenery, but "our own mountain home" furnishes much of interest to look at, if we could only find opportunities of visiting, and then appreciate the grandeur of nature near us. About three o'clock in the afternoon, we arrived at President Haight's dwelling, where we met my dear friend Louisa and her family; also Apostle F. D. Richards who had gone from Kelton to Oakley by stage. We were all weary from the effects of the journey, but were soon rested, and able to attend the conferences which convened the two ensuing days.

Elder Richards was quite poorly on Saturday and Sunday, yet was able to speak to the people, and gave them much good instruction. Many of the brethren and sisters from the different settlements had left their work, and come to the meetings, and a feeling of union seemed to prevail among the people. I had the pleasure of staying one night with my dear friend Sarah, also of eating dinner with Sister Julia Haight Smith, wife of Bishop John L. Smith, and daughter of Brother and Sister Haight. Our visit to Oakley was marred in a measure by the illness of Sister Haight, who could not leave her room the last two days of our stay. On Monday morning, September 22nd, we started for home. President Haight and Brother Loren Robinson took us in their carriages to Elba, one day's journey from Oakley. Stopping for dinner at the house of Counselor Brim who lives in Albion. Thus taking a different route on our return, for which we had reason to thank President Haight, as he wished us to see all of the country possible. An appointment was made for a meeting to be held at Elba in the evening, so the people of that place could have the privilege of hearing from Apostle Richards and the sisters. I met many of my old friends at the meeting, who had once lived in Farmington, which was quite a pleasing surprise to me. We put up for the night with the family of Bishop Taylor.

Some very painful incidents were called to my mind upon entering the settlement of Elba. The graves of Albert and Horton Smith were pointed out to us, two nephews of President Haight, who had lost their lives in one day while working on a new saw-mill; leaving their mother childless.

This was also the place where Sister Nancy A. Clark, a dear friend of mine, had come to minister to the wants of her son and his motherless children. Through exposure, and perhaps over work, she was prostrated with a severe illness, from which she never recovered. These things caused a sad feeling to come over me; but such is life. Some persons have much of sorrow and suffering, while others pass through life apparently in ease and comfort.

Brothers Haight and Robinson left us at Elba, and returned home. Brother Beecher took us on to Kelton, where we again took the cars. Arriving in Ogden Tuesday evening, we repaired to the house of Sister Josephine West, (daughter of Brother and Sister Richards,) and partook of a nice warm supper which she had provided. Wednesday the 24th, Sister Z. D. Young, and myself took train for home, which I reached at Farmington, feeling much benefitted by the journey and visits.

CHAPTER X.

BIBLE REFERENCES.—ANOTHER SURPRISE.

There are chapters in the Bible which took my particular attention when a little girl. The first is where Moses was called of the Lord to go into Egypt and deliver the children of Israel from bondage. (*Exodus, Chapters 3 and 4.*) His excusing himself on account of being slow of speech and not eloquent, and asking the Lord to send some one else, I used to wonder at. Why had Moses not faith when the Lord told him He would be with his mouth, and teach him what he should say? Since then I have been in places where I could understand the feelings of Moses better, and could truly sympathize with him.

The next place is where Elijah was about to ascend into heaven. (*Second Book of Kings, second chapter.*) Elijah wanted Elisha who was with him to tarry behind, but he would not, and therefore he saw Elijah ascend into heaven, thereby receiving what he desired, a double portion of the spirit of God.

This seemed to me one of the greatest boons that could be granted to man. And if any one should ask me what I would desire above all other things, if I could have my wish; the answer would be without any hesitation, a fullness of the Spirit of God, for that includes everything my heart could desire. To my mind there is nothing that can compare with the sweet and heavenly influence of the Holy Spirit. For this Spirit brings peace and happiness, and gives power to discern the thoughts and doings of men, and to know their results; as Elisha did when after healing the leper Naaman, his servant Gehazi told him a falsehood about the presents received; and we read of the curse that followed Gehazi for so doing. There are other passages that were equally important to my mind; but I will let this suffice.

Another interesting event in my life occurred on the 24th of June, 1892, which I feel it my duty to mention in gratitude to my friends, even though it refers to myself individually. An entertainment was prepared for my especial benefit. The young men and young women who had been the first members in the Primary Associations of Farmington were the leaders in the movement, which came about in the shape of another grand surprise. And this one excelled all others that had taken place before. Not that the workers were any more earnest, or that it could be more appreciated by me than those previously given, but it was on a grander scale, the meeting house being the place of resort. How well it was managed! Even the leading authorities of the ward were present; also the counselors of the Presidency of Davis Stake, one of whom was John W. Hess, our former Bishop. His face was one in particular (in connection with that of his wife, Julia) that I saw in one of the buggies as they drove up to our gate about 7 o'clock p. m., preceded by the Silver Band of Farmington, which was playing some lively strains. I was sitting on the porch and about to retire to my room, being feeble in health, when the procession drove up and

George Palmer and Daniel T. Miller—the originators of the plot—John Clark, Anna Clark Tanner, Kate Hinman Knowlton, Eva Clark and others came inside and said this was all for me, and they wished to escort me to the meeting house. I was like one in a dream, and was taken into the house, assisted by my daughters, Lucy and Leone, to have my things put on, where for a few moments I indulged in silent weeping. My daughter Ella had come up from Salt Lake City on the 4 o'clock train, to make a short visit, as I supposed. Just before leaving my room a greater surprise awaited me. Whom should I see but my sisters Ellen and Catherine, my son Orson, his wife and oldest daughter, who had also come from the City to do me honor. I rode to the meeting house with my husband in Mrs. Lucy A. Clark's carriage which was in waiting.

Upon arriving I was assisted by George Palmer up the steps and through the aisles of the meeting house, into the vestry, where tables were set, and most of the people were seated. I was placed beside Mrs. Helen M. Miller, one of my counselors in the first Primary. After supper was over we repaired to the main room in the building, where a program, which had been previously arranged, was carried out. Two addresses were given in the course of the evening, one by G. Palmer, and the other by D. T. Miller. A song composed for the occasion by Mrs. Lucy A. Clark, was read by Miss Eva Clark, and afterwards sung by herself and her sister Mamie.

SONG.

GREETING TO SISTER AURELIA S. ROGERS, BY LUCY A. CLARK.

(Tune, "Home of Our Youth," Found in the Juvenile Instructor, Sept., 1889, Vol. 24.)

A ship o'er life's ocean was sailing,
　Which brought to us tidings of joy;
A message from heaven to greet us,
　Glad tidings to each girl and boy.
It was brought by her whom we honor,
　In whose presence we mingle today,
With hearts filled with love and devotion,
　To cheer her on life's checkered way.

Chorus:

We honor thy dear name, thy works we revere,
　Our memories gratefully twine
Round the children's bright anchor established by thee,
　Which will now and eternally shine.

The Primary armies are marshalled in line,
　While they bless thee, Jehovah they praise,
The sweet songsters join in their anthems of joy
　For the mercies of these latter days.
They are marching with step firm and fearless,
　Bravely seeking the Lord in their youth,
The victory is theirs if they faithful remain
　And continue to struggle for truth.

Chorus:

The gold of the earth would be worthless,
　Compared with the truths you have taught,
A statue we rear while you're living,
　More sure than in marble well wrought.
If we heed the sweet counsel you've given,
　And practice it ever with care,
We will meet with our blessed Redeemer,
　And with love's tokens honor you there.

Chorus:

An essay was read by Mrs. Anna C. Tanner, which she had written for the occasion.

I had thought it unnecessary to give place to the essay here, as much of it would seem but a repetition of Primary History. But upon reconsideration, it seems to me a valuable testimony, strengthening that which has appeared before in behalf of the Primary cause. And for this intent a portion of it is included in this chapter.

ESSAY.

"In the year 1878, Sister Aurelia Rogers' motherly sympathy for the little children of Zion was so great that God inspired her with the idea of organizing them into an association. The first organization was effected in Farmington, August 11th, 1878. Many of us were present on that occasion, and have participated in the blessings and privileges derived therefrom. As children, we were very proud to have our own little meetings, for even then did we know that the interesting moral stories and encouraging words of Sister Rogers and her co-laborers made it easier for us to be obedient, to resist temptation, control our tempers, and keep the Sabbath day holy.

"The joy that we realized in becoming acquainted with the Spirit of God, the simple but honest resolutions that entered our minds, cannot be too highly appreciated. I think that I speak for all faithful members of the Primary, when I say that much of our happiness and prosperity, and ambition to become good and useful, is due to the valuable instructions and encouragement received in the Primary Association.

"Who of us have forgotten the impressive lessons taught us on the Word of Wisdom? The result of which is that whole families, grown, half-grown, and little sons and daughters can be found now, in which none use tea or coffee. Some have never tasted it, nor any kind of liquor; even in medicine it is refused. How many of us received our first lesson in singing in the Primary Association, and with what pride did the little boys, dressed in uniform, show their skill in playing the flute, etc.? No one will forget the first carpet made by the patient fingers of the little Primary girls. And the lessons of industry that were taught us in the bean patch will long be remembered with pride and pleasure. The concerts and fairs were our delight.

"What a broad field of usefulness was presented to us, but still so gradually was it opened to our view that every new feature brought with it renewed ambition."

* * * * *

Speeches were made by Brother Jacob Miller and by Stake Counselor, Hyrum Grant. After which a picture of flowers in a large frame was presented to me from the committee, with appropriate remarks.

I shall never forget the feeling of awe and humility that came over me while being assisted into the stand to express my thanks. The committee, who occupied the stand, were sitting as I entered, but upon a given signal, they arose to their feet and remained standing while I spoke a few words. My presence of mind nearly deserted me at this last move, it was so unexpected.

The honor given me was equal to that given to a queen upon a throne, and the question arose from my heart, have I deserved all this?

After the exercises were over, I was escorted to the carriage by D. T. Miller, when, after a few minutes' ride I was at my home again. My mind was so full of what had transpired during the evening, that I could not close my eyes in sleep until nearly morning.

On the 27th I wrote the following, and forwarded it to the head committee:

"To the Committee, and all those who took part in effecting the surprise given me on the 24th of this month.

"I have not words to express my feelings in regard to the movement. It was indeed a complete surprise, for the thought had not entered my mind nor my heart, that such a thing could ever come to pass. It gives me joy unspeakable to think that those who were once under my charge as members in the first Primary Association, and who have since grown to manhood and womanhood, should remember me with so much love and respect. Eventful day! A day that will be spoken of in years to come. Not that I desire to have homage paid me, nor to be the center of all eyes, for I naturally shrink from anything of the kind. But to know that I have the love and good will of the people, both old and young, is indeed a precious boon, more to be prized than all the world besides. One thing I felt to regret was the labor and expense which naturally comes in getting up anything so grand, for it was indeed grand.

"The supper table in a room beautifully decorated, the numerous flower-pots and bouquets, the music of the band, the lovely present, a picture of flowers encased in a beautiful frame; a well-arranged program which was heaven-inspired. Yes, was it not inspiration that caused one or two persons (George Palmer and Daniel T. Miller) to think of such a move, and others join heart and hand with a united effort, in order that one poor, weak human being, who had been afflicted in body and mind for some time past, might be made happy.

"Please accept my heartfelt thanks, and may the blessings of heaven attend you every one; and my prayers will continually ascend to the Throne of Grace in your behalf.

"Yours Affectionately,

"AURELIA S. ROGERS."

This surprise happened to take place on the fortieth birthday of my oldest child, Orson.

※ ※ ※

CHAPTER XI.

MEMBERS OF THE FIRST PRIMARY ASSOCIATION.—REFLECTION.

THE suggestion comes to my mind very forcibly to have the names of the members in the first Primary copied into this book just as we received them in our visit around the Ward. Their names are set down according to the districts they lived in; their ages I will omit. Some persons may think it unnecessary to copy so many names but I do not look at it so. Are they not my children in one sense of the word? Does not every President who is engaged in Primary work have her heart drawn out with love towards those under her care? Then are we not all to be judged from the books? We understand that we are; and are also instructed to take great care in preserving our records.

DISTRICT NO. 1.

Hyrum Christensen
Hyrum Rice
David Rice
John Rice
James Glover
David Glover
Jefferson Kent
Hyrum S. Kent
John S. White
Schuyler White

Nora E. Glover
Mena Lund
Sarah Floyd
Adelaide White
Joanna Kent
Martha Rice
Mary Rice
Ethelynn Rice
Harriet Rice
Emma Rice

Mena Christensen

DISTRICT NO. 2.

William Hardy
John E. Pierce
Alonzo Pierce
Edward Pierce

Alice Smith
Maggie Smith
Susan Steed
Vilate Steed

David Hughes
Solomon Hughes
David Goodyear
Truman Goodyear
Franklin Steed
D. Albert Oviott
George Stayner
Chancey Haight
Gertrude Stayner
Kate Stayner

Louna Rice
Nettie Sides
Flossie Sides
Josephine Oviott
Nannie Oviott
May Turner
Hattie Hardy
Julia Haight
Alice L. Haight
Alice Steed

DISTRICT NO. 3.

William Cotterell
Joseph Cotterell
James H. Robinson
Charles Lewis Robinson
Heber Butters
Frank Lamb
Laban Smith
Loren Walker
Joseph Walker
Don Carlos Walker

Mark E. Walker
Charles Walker
Frank Hinman
Ann Maria Lamb
Lucy J. Lamb
Eada Smith
Catherine Smith
Esther Smith
Lucy A. Robinson
Mamie Robinson

Kate Cotterell

DISTRICT NO. 4.

Ezra J. Smith
Joseph D. Burnett
Samuel H. Burnett

Eugene Clark
Ezra Robinson
Anna Clark

LIFE SKETCHES.

John W. Steed
William Steed
Joseph Steed
Levi Tippetts
John J. Tippetts
Amasa Clark
John Clark

Sarah Clark
Alice Clark
Eva Clark
Mamie Clark
Rosabel Robinson
Celia Smith
Martha Jones

DISTRICT NO. 5.

William Millard
Hyrum P. Workman
John S. Workman
Hector Haight
Edward A. Stevenson
Wilford Stevenson
Ernest Walker

Lucy I. Rogers
Leone Rogers
Mary Haight
Anna Haight
Margaret Jones
Sarah J. Robinson
Anna Robinson

Fanny Workman

DISTRICT NO. 6.

Thomas H. Gleason
Stanley Dallin
Joseph Robinson
Oliver Wilcox
David E. Wilcox
William H. Glover
Seymour Miller
Lyman Miller
Elmer Rose
Frederick Coombs

William J. Coombs
James C. Coombs
Eliza Gleason
Margaret R. Wilcox
Alice C. Glover
Rosa Walker
Lucy M. Walker
Eva Miller
Agnes Coombs
Clarabel Rose

DISTRICT NO. 7.

George Palmer
Ambrose Palmer
Ezra Palmer
Nephi Palmer
William F. Grover
Enoch Grover
Edward Bigler
James Bigler
Daniel T. Miller
Edwin Smith

Dueane Haight
Isaac Haight
Minnie Palmer
Emma Palmer
Alcetta Burk
Emma Grover
Zernah Grover
Polly Grover
Athalia Miller
Alice Smith

DISTRICT NO. 8.

Joseph H. Cotterell
James W. Cotterell
Wilford Richards
Willard Vanfleet
Willard Peart
Lewis E. Abbott
Frederick W. Richards
Lanson Vanfleet
Dewey Vanfleet

Rosabel Vanfleet
Sylvia Vanfleet
Zina Vanfleet
Hannah Wilson
Annetta Smith
Laura L. Smith
Beatrice Vanfleet
Martha Cotterell
Rebecca Cotterell

Rhumina Chaffin

DISTRICT NO. 9.

David C. Hess
John W. Hess, Jr.

Clara A. Leonard
Hattie A. Leonard

LIFE SKETCHES

Wilford Hess
Frank Hess
John Preece
Scott Preece
Leonidas Kennard

Mary E. Hess
Sarah J. Hess
Alice M. Hess
Adeline Hess
Susie Vanfleet

May Kennard

DISTRICT NO. 10.

William Clawson
John Clawson
Howard Hinman
Lewis M Hinman
Henry Hollist
John T. Hollist

Emmeline Hess
Lucy White
Katie White
Kate Hinman
May Hinman
Jesse Mayfield

Sarah J. Tubbs

DISTRICT NO. 11.

William Barrett
Peter Duncan
George M. Leonard
Truman J. Leonard
Andrew Udy
Charles A. Udy
Henry Moon
Edmund Moon
Osron Moon

Armond Moon
Philip Moon
Rose A. Williams
Martha M. Barrett
Mary Duncan
Jane Duncan
Anna Duncan
Amy Leonard
Rowena Moon

DISTRICT NO. 12.

Jacob Workman

Thomas Workman

David E. Manning	Lucy A. Jeffs
William H. Manning	Elizabeth Jeffs
Moroni Secrist	Josephine Workman
Edwin Secrist	Alice J. Workman
George Secrist	Elizabeth Manning
Ursel S. Rose	Alvira Welling
Armond Rose	Eliza Jane Clark
Franklin D. Welling	Eliza S. Clark
Joseph Welling	Maria A Clark
John A. Bourne	Anna Clark
George A. Bourne	Esther Clark

One hundred and twelve boys and one hundred and twelve girls. Total two hundred and twenty-four.

There may possibly have been some names omitted or some misspelled; if so, it has not been intentional. As far as I can learn, only six deaths had occurred among this large number of children, up to 1892. Yet very many of them have moved away from Farmington.

In connection with Primary work, there are certain things upon which I will offer a few of my views. They are matters which I feel we cannot be too diligent in teaching to the young or in reflecting upon and holding to ourselves.

My mind is drawn out, and I am perhaps over anxious, (if such a thing could be,) for the welfare of my children, and for all human beings, desiring that they may live pure lives and prepare themselves while here, for a better life beyond. This is a preparatory state that we are in, as I understand it, and our happiness in the next world depends very much upon how we conduct ourselves in this. These things are clearly explained in the Book of Alma, chapter forty-two, (Book of Mormon.)

In the first place we are not perfect beings; if we had no faults ourselves, we would perhaps have no charity for those who do have them. I think the Lord permits us sometimes to do things contrary to our better judgment that we may have charity for others. We are passing through an experience and have the good and the evil placed before us so that we can choose for ourselves which to accept. There are not many persons probably, who think they are choosing the evil; how are they to know? We are told that there are two spirits that influence our lives, the good and the bad. The good spirit is from God, and brings peace and happiness; makes us feel to love others as ourselves and try to make them happy; while the bad spirit tends to make people miserable. The good spirit carries with it a feeling of forgiveness, so that if others injure us in any way, we will hold no hard feelings but do them a good turn when we can; thus showing the nobility of the soul which does not stoop to do mean acts, and return evil for evil. This good spirit assists us when we are passing through trials or having deep sorrow, which trials and sorrows are necessary in order to prove whether we will trust in God to the end. If this spirit is present when death is in the house it brings a feeling of peace so that you do not realize that death is there. There are times when all is dark and gloomy, and apparently nothing to look forward to. Perhaps the husband or wife has been taken away by death; or their darling children have been snatched from them, in some cases three or four in one week, until their heart strings are wrung almost beyond endurance, and they cannot see the hand of God in it, any more than

Job's friends could understand why he was so afflicted. For the Lord permitted Satan to tempt Job, as we read in the Book of Job, (Bible.)

There are persons who have been afflicted financially, their means have been swept away from them through some cause, or other trouble is weighing them down. At such times the evil spirit may have such an influence that many are tempted to take their own lives, and suicide may be committed. In all trying cases there is need to go to the Lord in mighty prayer, and if your prayers are not answered speedily, continue your supplications; ask Him to help you out of trouble; then have faith enough to believe that He will, in His own time and way. And if the Lord condescends to let His Holy Spirit (which is the Comforter) rest upon you, your heart will indeed be cheered. But if He seems to withhold His blessings and your prayers are not answered in the way you desire, can you feel to acknowledge His hand even in this, and say Thy will be done and not mine? This is what I call trusting in God.

Many times I have been comforted in hearing the hymn, "How firm a foundation, ye Saints of the Lord," especially the 4th and 5th verses which I will copy.

"When through the deep waters I call thee to go,
The rivers of sorrow shall not thee o'erflow;
For I will be with thee, thy troubles to bless,
And sanctify to thee thy deepest distress.

"When through fiery trials thy pathway shall lie,
My grace, all sufficient, shall be thy supply;
The flame shall not hurt thee; I only design
Thy dross to consume and thy gold to refine."

※ ※ ※

CHAPTER XII.

A DREAM—FURTHER TESTIMONIES OF APPRECIATION.

NEARLY four years ago this book was, as I thought, ready for publication. But owing to financial depression all through the country, I was advised to wait until times were more favorable; it was therefore laid aside.

About that time I had a singular dream, and although I do not in a general way pay much attention to dreams, this one impressed me deeply.

I thought that my sister Ellen and myself were on the side of a steep mountain trying to ascend; but on account of its steepness, we had to cling to the shrubbery for support. When my dream opened I found myself in this condition, with sister Ellen a little south of me. I noticed that she grasped at the bushes on the side hill, and struggled with all her might to make some headway; yet our progress was slow indeed. I turned my head and looked back into the valley below; saw the houses and fields, which looked peaceful in the distance and I felt a longing to be there; when something seemed to whisper to me that I must stop looking back, or I would never be able to reach the top of the mountain. Not to look back was hard at first, but I made the effort and succeeded in overcoming the temptation. Glancing over to my sister I found that she had stopped; the last I saw of her she was straining every nerve to advance, but to no purpose. After she stopped, I went on fast and soon gained the top.

Looking around me I saw mountains and peaks without end, but none of them were higher than the one that I had climbed. I was viewing these mountains with wonder, when I awoke.

What is the interpretation of the dream? was the question I asked myself over and over again.

At that time I was in considerable worry of mind over things that had passed; did my dream mean that I should not reflect on these things, but look forward to the future? Why did sister Ellen stop, and I go forward? I thought that one of us would die; but which one? My health was poor, while sister Ellen was fairly well. She would perhaps stay and I would go to the other side. A few years told the story. Sister Ellen was soon taken ill, she lingered and suffered for nearly three years, and then died.

What does reaching the top of the mountain mean? Can it be the publication of my book, and Primary work? This interpretation only came to my mind lately. My sisters, Ellen and Catharine and myself had often talked over the publishing of the book, trying to solve the problem of how it could be done. I thought possibly it might not be accomplished in my lifetime. Ellen said she believed it would; and her faith strengthened my own, which was somewhat wavering.

Again, Ellen and I were both engaged in Primary work, struggling to make progress, but the advance was slow. The mountains and peaks seen in my dream might be compared to the Primary work without end.

When my book was nearly completed, I began to reflect as to whom I could find to assist me in getting the manuscript ready for the printers. Different persons came to my mind, and finally the name of Sister Lula Greene Richards presented itself, and was accepted. In starting out on my errand, going from my son Orson's house on 3rd Street, to the home of Sister Richards, which is only a few blocks farther east, there was a steep hill to climb. In ascending this hill my dream came to my mind which confirmed my opinion that I was in the right direction, and that Sister Richards was the one to help me.

Since Sister Ellen's death the way seems to be opening, and I feel that she is assisting me on the other side.

When President Louie B. Felt first heard that I had written a book, the subject was brought before the General Board of the Primary, and all the sisters present were anxious to see it in print. Steps were taken as soon as practicable to bring this about. Sister Felt and her Counselors, Sisters, Lillie T. Freeze and Josephine R. West and their Secretary, Sister May Anderson were prompt, energetic, and indefatigable in their united efforts to have the work accomplished. Letters were sent (without my knowledge) to every Primary Association, explaining the matter and asking their assistance. Suggesting that the 11th of August, the day on which the first Primary Presidents were set apart, be kept as the birthday of the Primary; and that on the coming August, the Presidents were to get up some kind of an entertainment. A program suitable for the occasion was prepared by the General Board and forwarded to each Association with the request that they donate the means received on that day after expenses were paid, as a present to Sister Rogers, for the publishing of her book. There was a hearty response in favor of the request as shown by the many letters forwarded to Sister Felt. And here, once more, I desire to express my gratitude—to tell that my heart goes out in thankfulness to my Heavenly Father and to the dear sisters and children who have been instruments in His hands of bringing this book before the world. Whatever good may come of it, my desire is that it shall be for the furtherance of Primary interests, and to the honor and glory of God. That the means so generously subscribed by the Primaries may be "like bread cast upon the waters," which shall return unto them increased and enriched.

About three weeks after Sister Ellen's death, my husband died suddenly of a paralytic stroke.

For a short time afterwards, I was prostrated with weakness and an overtaxed mind. But what surprised me greatly was that I soon rallied, and was comforted in a great degree. I knew Primary children were praying for me, but not until a few weeks later did I receive particular testimony. Sister L. L. G. Richards had taken a trip to the southern part of Utah, to visit the Associations. She heard of my husband's death and told them about it, and while in Richfield, a special prayer was offered up in my behalf in Primary Conference. This was no doubt the case in other places, and I received the benefit; and I thank the children everywhere who remembered me in that way.

> Little children, how I love them,
>   Pure, bright spirits from above;
> What would heaven be without them?
>   Or this world, without their love?
>
> Yet these little angel spirits,
>   Sometimes have been heard to say
> Naughty words, use impure language,
>   While in anger at their play.
>
> Little thinking of the Tempter,
>   Ever, ever, standing near,
> Waiting, watching to mislead them,
>   From the ways of truth, I fear.

Then dear children be ye always
  Pure and holy day by day;
Ask the Lord to guard and keep you,
  In the straight and narrow way.

Never grieve your Heavenly Watchers,
  By a coarse or impure word;
Nor forget to pray for loved ones,
  For the children's prayers are heard.

❧ ❧ ❧

CHAPTER XIII.

LOVED ONES GONE BEFORE.

The following extracts are from the *Woman's Exponent*, written by the Editor, Sister Emmeline B. Wells.

ELLEN CURTIS SPENCER CLAWSON.

*　　*　　*　　*　　*　　*　　*

"The sister whose demise we now record was a dear friend of bye-gone days, and her death calls up many reminiscences and experiences of the past. A true and sincere friend at all times and in all places was Sister Ellen C. Clawson; her life has been a noble example from her childhood until her spirit took its flight from earth to a brighter realm. Her last moments, just previous to her departure, were singularly calm and peaceful. One of her daughters remarked to the writer that she was quite sure her mother had an escort to accompany her to the spirit world.

"Sister Clawson's death occurred August 25th, 1896. Her husband and all her children were gathered around her bedside, where she lay perfectly conscious and, as ever during her life, thoughtful of every one but herself. Her faculties of mind were bright and active until the last when her beautiful gentle spirit departed from this world to join the innumerable hosts of Saints who have gone before.

"Sister Clawson was of New England parentage. Her grandfather, Daniel Spencer, served in the Revolutionary war.

*　　*　　*　　*　　*　　*　　*

"As a child and a young girl Miss Spencer endeared herself to a host of young people to whom she has always been strongly attached, though many of them have passed on before her. She was baptized at nine years of age in the Mississippi River at Nauvoo.   *   *   *

"In March 1850 Miss Spencer was united in marriage to Hiram B. Clawson, a very popular young man in Salt Lake at that time, and since then well known here and elsewhere in mercantile and other business affairs. He has been for several years past bishop of the Twelfth ward of this city. Mrs. Clawson has been the mother of fourteen children, nine of whom are still living, and she has numerous grandchildren. She was almost idolized by her own family, which cannot be wondered at when one considers how particularly unselfish her whole life has been. Although extremely diffident in all public affairs, yet because of her intense devotion to her religion, she accepted positions that brought her into prominence in women's organizations. In April, 1879, she was elected to preside over the Primary Association in the Twelfth ward, and June 19th, 1880, she was called and set apart at a Conference held in the Assembly Hall in this city, to preside over the Primary Association in the Salt Lake Stake.

This office she has filled with honor and to the entire satisfaction of all interested parties ever since. She had a particular gift in this direction, and with her Counselors has traveled in this Stake, organizing and encouraging the labors of the sisters and the advancement of the children as much as possible for sixteen years. She is greatly beloved by the children all through this Stake of Zion, and wherever she is known.

* * * * * * *

"Her loss will be deeply felt in the community where she has labored so faithfully, as well as by her own particular friends and family. The writer herself feels deeply the loss of her society and friendship, but fully realizes that her lovely character, her pure life and her integrity to the Gospel, have entitled her to the exaltation for which she lived and sacrificed, and that her joy now is beyond expression. Jesus said 'It hath not entered into the heart of man to conceive the glory our Father hath in store for them that love him.'"

"Thou art not with the dead
  Whose earth in the earth we lay,
While the bearers softly tread,
  And the mourners kneel and pray;
From thy semblance dumb and stark,
  The soul has taken its flight—
Out of the finite dark,
  Into the infinite light."

THOUGHTS, ON THE DEATH OF MRS. ELLEN C. CLAWSON, BY LYDIA D. ALDER.

August 25th, 1896.

"At a gathering of the sisters in the home of the writer on July 2nd, 1896, while speaking, Sister Clawson said, 'I sing in my heart all the time, and sometimes I could shout for very joy, I feel so happy; but I never was a singer.'

"On resuming her seat, Sister Zina D. H. Young, the president of the Relief Society who presided at the meeting, uttered the following prophetic words, 'Sister Clawson, you shall sing until your heart is satisfied; you shall be one of the sweetest singers when you go beyond the Veil."

"Sing, dear one sing, and shout for very joy!
In the world above the stars, where strife cannot annoy.
Thy heart so full of heavenly joy, shall now be satisfied;
And in His presence thou wilt bask, who for us bled and died,
And tho' we drop the tear of love, and sigh that thou art gone;
Yet joy is bubbling uppermost, that thou a crown hast won.
Faithful unto death! Thy Covenant vows unbroke;
And singing in thy heart the song the Gospel sound awoke;
O, who would shrink the burden, when the crown is sure to come?
'Who bears the cross, will wear the crown,' the prophets all
    have sung:
Brave hearts, true hearts, who walk the way in tears,
And only trace the journey by the slowly changing years,
Be comforted! though strife and sorrow too, be rife;
Hear thro' the gloom and darkness, 'I am the Resurrection and
    the Life.'
Dear one adieu! adieu! But O! 'twill not be long,
Till we who mourn thee now, must learn the changing song;
For fairer in the East dawns the Resurrection morn—
The grave will yield its sleepers up, and of its power be shorn.
Thou in thy snowy robes, gems sparkling on thy brow,—
The past beneath thy feet, and only pleasure now,—
Wilt in thy shining mansion, that ever will be home,
Throw open wide the portals, and bid thy loved ones 'Come.'"

LIFE SKETCHES.

MOTHER.

Words and Music by Georgie Clawson Foote.
Arranged by Spencer Clawson, Jr.

How sad the scene that's now be-fore us, Our moth-er dear, to lay a-way; But
And on the morrow when she wak-ens, Her soul and bod-y will u-nite, And

DEATH OF ELDER THOMAS ROGERS.

FROM THE DAVIS COUNTY CLIPPER.

*　　*　　*　　*　　*

"Thomas Rogers, whose death occurred on the 16th of September, 1896, was not only one of the early settlers of Farmington, but one of the old timers, and was intimately acquainted with the Prophet Joseph Smith, having had the privilege of eating and sleeping with him. * * * Deceased was born in October 1827, at Falkirk, Scotland, and while very young moved with his parents to Canada, and subsequently to Kirtland and Nauvoo. He shared with the Saints in all their moves, arriving in Salt Lake City in the fall of 1848. * * * Of the seven children now living, all except his son Andrew L., who was called to settle in Arizona many years ago, were present at his funeral. * * * The pallbearers were his half brother, William Lamoreaux, Spencer Clawson, B. S. Young and his three sons, Orson, George and Curtis." * * *

FROM THE DESERET NEWS.

"The funeral services over the remains of Elder Thomas Rogers were held at the family residence, in Farmington, Friday morning. A large concourse of friends and relatives were in attendance. The deceased was one of the early settlers of this country and many of the pioneers were there to pay their last respects to their old friend and comrade.

"The services were presided over by Bishop Secrist. The Farmington Ward choir rendered the hymn, 'The Resurrection Day,' which was followed by an invocation by Elder C. W. Stayner. Mrs Dora Robinson sang Eliza R. Snow's beautiful hymn, 'O my Father.' Bishop Secrist was the first speaker. He paid a tribute to the integrity of Brother Rogers whom he had known for many years, and whom he had always found ready to perform whatsoever was asked of him. Elder John W. Hess addressed remarks of consolation to the bereaved family and paid further tributes to the departed one, whose life here on earth had been one of "peace and good will to all men." Elder Brigham Young of the Council of the Apostles then addressed the mourners and friends; he had been associated with Brother Rogers in the earlier history of the Church as a missionary to Europe and also as an Indian fighter, Brother Rogers having been one of the trusty minute men of Utah's early days. In the course of his remarks Elder Young set forth the hope of the Latter-day Saints as regards their dead, and referred to death as being rather the 'inception and not the destruction of life.' In closing he said, 'Brother Thomas Rogers has gone to meet his God; to rest with the righteous and the faithful who have gone before. The lesson we learn in this is, 'Be ye also ready.' He closed his tribute to the memory of the dead by invoking God's choicest blessings upon the living.

"A quartette composed of Mrs Dora Robinson, soprano, Miss Mamie Clark, contralto, Nephi O. Palmer, Tenor, and Jos. E. Robinson, basso, very artistically rendered 'I Need Thee Every Hour.'

"The benediction was pronounced by Elder

Jacob Miller. The remains were taken to Salt Lake City this afternoon for interment, where the mother of Elder Rogers is buried."———

On the 20th of January following my husband's death, little Roger E. Avery, ten months old, my daughter Lucy's only child, died after an illness of five weeks. Lucy had been to Farmington to see her father in his last sickness. When she came to the bedside, he noticed the baby in her arms and put up his hand as if to play with it. It seemed singular, we thought, for previously he had paid very little attention to any of us. The precious little one following so soon after its grandfather, caused us to think that there must have been a bond between them which death was not long to separate.

LINES BY L. L. GREENE RICHARDS.

AFFECTIONATELY INSCRIBED TO SISTER AURELIA S. ROGERS ON THE DEATH OF HER HUSBAND, ELDER THOMAS ROGERS.

"'True until death!' Can more be said?
Unto all those who weepeth,
May we not say of the blessed dead,
'He is not dead, but sleepeth?'

Sleepeth to waken, glad and young,
  When the song of the blest redeemed is sung.

Though the vail of death to mortal view
  Seemeth forever clouded,
The spirit home of the just and true
  Cannot be darkly shrouded.
We should see, could the vail but be withdrawn,
  A realm of light where our friend hath gone.

Husband and father, gone before,
  Thou leavest thy loved ones to mourn for thee:
Whilst thou preparest a place once more,
  That where thou art they may also be;
Than earth home brighter and better far,
  In the house where the many mansions are.

But God regardeth the widow's tear,
  Our Father heareth the orphan's moan;
Oh! wife beloved, and children dear,
  Look up in faith; ye are not alone!
May the Comforter guide ye safely o'er,
  To the home of the loved ones gone before.

CHAPTER XIV.

PRIMARIES IN BOX ELDER AND CACHE STAKES.

During the few years that my manuscript was laid away in a place of safety, my life work was going on just the same. Many things occurred to make me feel joyful and happy, while others were of a sorrowful nature and are best not dwelt much upon. Cheerfulness and pleasant thoughts help to produce longevity, and are traits that should be cultivated. A favorite motto with me is "Always look on the bright side of everything," and if anything has been written in these pages of an opposite nature, it was because it seemed necessary.

In these years of waiting, I have had many privileges; have attended Primary Conferences in other stakes than our own; also visited the City of Washington, the great Capitol of the United States of America.

These trips I will touch briefly upon, as they have filled niches in my life's history that cannot well be passed over without notice. On the 12th of June, 1893, I visited a Primary Conference in Brigham City, Box Elder Co., which was conducted under the able management of President Alvira Reese and her assistants, Nephena Madsen and Amelia Graehl; went to the Opera House in the evening and listened to an excellent program, rendered by the children of the different wards. I stopped in Brigham City a few days visiting relatives and friends, among whom were the families of President Rudger Clawson and Brother Nathan Cheney. Also visited Willard City, after which I accompanied Sister Lillie T. Freeze to Logan, Cache County. Sister Freeze had come to Brigham City to attend the Young Ladies' Conference and was going to Cache in the interest of the Primary. At the depot in Logan we were met by Counselor Mattie Hansen, who took us to her home where we enjoyed her hospitality. The next day, on the 19th, attended the Stake Primary Conference, where we met President

Jane Molen, and her other Counselor, Emma Pike.

Went with Brother and Sister Molen, in the evening to their home in Hiram. Brother Simpson M. Molen is one of the Presidency in the Cache Valley Stake. The brethren spared no pains to make our visits through their valley enjoyable, traveling with us from place to place, and also attending our meetings.

While in Cache, I met many early acquaintances. Elder Orson Smith, President of Cache Stake, when quite young lived neighbor to us in Farmington. Also Sister Anna Hansen, who presides over the Wellsville Primary was born in Farmington, next door to us. Brother William Hendricks and his wife Alvira of Richmond, were our Nauvoo neighbors.

At the home of Sister Hansen in Wellsville, where Sister Freeze and I stayed all night, I was quite ill for a few hours, and retired early. President Jane Molen was also there having come so far, on her visit through the county. In the evening I was startled with hearing the sweetest singing and music imaginable, which proceeded from another room of the house. Brother Hansen and his wife, assisted by others of his household, and the visitors, were the choir. They sang several hymns, with organ accompaniment; but when the words "Nearer my God to Thee," fell upon my ear, I felt that I was in a realm like unto Heaven, and that I was indeed near to my God.

※ ※ ※

CHAPTER XV.

VISITS TO ATLANTA, GEORGIA, AND WASHINGTON, D. C.

IN endeavoring to touch briefly upon the incidents connected with my visits to the above named places, I find that two lengthy chapters are the result. And yet it seems that little has been said, for so much has been left out that is of great interest to me.

In November, 1894, I was nominated and elected delegate to a Woman's Suffrage Convention, to be held in the City of Atlanta,

Georgia. This honor was conferred at a convention held in Farmington, by the delegates of the Woman's Suffrage Association of Davis County. Not only did my friends sustain me by their votes, but they generously provided the necessary means to pay all the expenses of the occasion.

Accordingly on the 26th of January, 1895, I left Salt Lake City, by train, for the East, in company with Mrs. Emmeline B. Wells, of Salt Lake City, President of the Woman's Suffrage Association of Utah, and Mrs. Marilla Daniels of Provo, delegate to the convention from Utah County. Our trip across the plains was a pleasant one, and quite different to the one taken many years ago, when we came to the Valley with ox teams. We passed through cities, and saw many fine buildings; in other places the country looked like a dense forest of trees, among which were some little huts set upon blocks for foundations; these huts were mostly occupied by colored people. Memories of the past were awakened as we crossed the Mississippi River on a bridge three-fourths of a mile long. This same river I had crossed over on a ferry boat about fifty years ago, at the time the Saints were driven from Nauvoo. As we neared the Eastern States, the lay of the country looked quite familiar, although I had never been over the same ground before. The hills, valleys and forests must have been similar to those I had traversed when a child; for often my little playmates and myself have taken our baskets and gone berrying, as there were all kinds of wild fruit growing in abundance; such as blackberries, strawberries, whortleberries, and wintergreen berries. Walnuts, hickorynuts, hazelnuts, etc., were also very plentiful. Many a time in Middlefield I have gone into the maple groves, after the trees had been tapped, and with a dipper drank of the sap before it was put into a kettle that hung over a fire close by, to be boiled down into syrup, or made into sugar.

After a journey of three days and a half, we arrived in the City of Atlanta, where we were met at the depot, by two ladies and a gentleman. (Previous to this our badges of yellow ribbon had been put on.) One of the ladies came up to me and asked if I were Susan B. Anthony. She was informed to the contrary, and I wondered if there could be a resemblance between us, and whether I ought to feel complimented. The same evening I met Miss Anthony for the first time, in the Committee room of the Aragon, the hotel to which our escort had taken us upon our arrival. Miss Anthony is tall and thin, wears glasses and is not very handsome, so I thought I might look like her; but when she smiled, and began talking to the ladies, the expression of her face was lovely. And the next day at the Convention, she walked with such grace, and presided with such dignity, that I felt quite honored with the possible resemblance.

The Committee meetings of the Woman's Suffrage Association, held in the Aragon were numerous. Mrs. Daniels was a member of the Executive Committee and I of the Committee on Resolutions.

The Aragon hotel is a building six stories high. Sister Daniels and myself took a room on the fourth floor, Sister Wells taking one adjoining ours, which she occupied alone. We went to and from our room on the elevator. There was one window but no outside view to the room, and it was lit up with electric light. The waiters, both men and women, were colored; when we wanted hot water, we gave three rings of the bell, two for ice water, and one if a boy were wanted.

We attended two and three meetings in the De Gives Opera House every day of the week that we remained in Atlanta. Many of the lady speakers were eloquent, and a spirit of kindness and good will prevailed. They were advocating the cause of humanity, and wanted the poor and suffering looked after. Among the speakers were many distinguished women of whom I had read and heard much, but had never hoped to have the pleasure of seeing and hearing personally.

Sunday forenoon I visited the Unitarian Church. After the services the privilege was given for any one to speak. A number of gentlemen and ladies from other places responded. I also spoke and told them I was from Utah. This immediately aroused curiosity, and many questions were asked concerning our people, which I answered to the best of my ability. In the afternoon, heard the Rev. Anna Shaw preach to an immense audience, and was much interested. In the evening, attended a reception in the parlors of the Aragon, where there was a general time of introducing and handshaking. Had the honor of speaking to the Governor of Georgia.

On the 5th, visited Decator, a city seven miles from Atlanta. Returning, passed by a cemetery where hundreds of soldiers were buried and a great battle fought at the time of the Civil War. Saw a place where there had been a skirmish, and a spy had been captured and hung. I listened to the recital of these things with peculiar feelings; to think I was passing over ground where such terrible scenes had been enacted.

The next day in the afternoon, took train for Washington, D. C., where we arrived early on the morning of the 7th; stopped at the depot where President Garfield was shot. Saw the very spot where he fell, which was marked by a star on the floor.

Our business in Washington was to attend the Second Triennial Congress of the National Council of Women. On our way, in looking for rooms for lodging, we passed through Central Market which is one block long, and full of everything imaginable to eat. Sister Daniels and I engaged a room of Mrs. M. F. Palmer, 710, 11th Street; Sister Wells stopped with some relations of hers, a Mr. and Mrs. Hall. Our room was on the second floor, had three windows, and was warmed by a register. As the Congress would not open until the 18th of February, we took advantage of the intervening time to visit the most noted places in the city. Every Sabbath we attended some Church. The first one visited in Washington was the Baptist Church Sunday School; the School was graded the same as ours in Utah. There were over six hundred in attendance. On our way home, stopped at the Lutheran Church and listened to the services; the singing in both places was fine.

Since leaving home we had realized the hand of Providence in our journeyings, and felt that we were being watched over by an unseen power. I myself had many evidences of this. When going to our meeting one evening, my hand bag which was on my arm, must have slipped off and fallen to the pavement; for a gentleman from behind walked up, and handing me the bag, asked if it was mine? When I saw it, my heart was in my mouth for a moment at the thought of its probable loss, for the sidewalk was crowded with people. I thanked the man for his kindness, and took good care not to lose it again. Aside from what the bag contained, it was a treasure in itself, and was doubly precious, having been handed to me by my dear niece, Lucy Grant, just before my leaving Salt Lake City.

On Monday the 11th of February we received another evidence. Sister Daniels and I, had put on our things with the intention of visiting the Capitol, when the lady of the house came in with a card from a gentleman below who wished to see us. I went down stairs, and Mr. Hall introduced himself; hearing of us from Mrs. Wells, he had called to make our acquaintance. Upon learning where we were going, he volunteered his services as pilot, which were thankfully accepted. The street car took us to the Congressional Library building, which is unfinished inside. This building is next to the Capitol and takes up one block of ground. We went down into the lower rooms, and saw the enormous pipes that heat the whole house; also the furnaces with a clock and thermometer over each one, so the heat can be regulated. The building is fire proof, everything is made of brick, stone, iron and marble; the only bit of wood we saw was the window sash; there were thousands of little shelves in preparation for books. From here we went to the Capitol, Mr. Hall guiding us through the different rooms, for he seemed to understand everything, and pleasantly explained things to us. Upon entering the grand rotunda in the center of the building, we sat down to rest, yet the gentleman, who was over seventy years of age, did not appear weary with his walking. After resting, Mr. Hall took us into the gallery that overlooks the Senate Chamber, while the Senate was in session; and we heard Mr. Blackburn, who had the floor, discuss the railroad question. Was it not wonderful that we should have such a privilege? If Mr. Hall had not been with us, we never could have gained access to certain rooms, especially a private library, where quite a number of persons were reading and none were permitted to speak a loud word, or scarcely whisper. In this room our attention was called to the original Bible that Martin Luther translated into German. A few days later, we visited this same building again, as we had a desire to enter the House of Representatives, which was in the south wing of the Capitol. When we called, there was much confusion; quite different to the Senate when we visited it. The man in the chair kept rapping the gavel on the table for order, but the men took little or no notice of it. I afterward went within seventy feet of the top of the dome, that being as far as we could go, I was a little too late to make the ascent with a company of ladies, and sister Daniels not feeling able to go with me, I went alone rather than be disappointed. In coming down the stairs I missed the door I started from and kept on going down till I reached the basement, when I was piloted to the room above, feeling very weary, having climbed three hundred and forty-eight steps, making six hundred and ninety-six steps going and coming.

A day or two after we called on Mr. and Mrs. Hall, and had lunch with them. Afterwards went to a large printing house, which is five stories high. There are six hundred girls employed in this building, besides a large number of men. I was informed that the machinery that prints on both sides at once, cost $100,000.

CHAPTER XVI.

THE WHITE HOUSE—THE WASHINGTON MONUMENT—COUNCIL MEETINGS—MOUNT VERNON—HOME AGAIN.

Among the important buildings visited was the White House. By starting early, Sister Daniels and I had the privilege of going through the main rooms of the house. The first one of importance that we entered is the East room; I called it the golden room as the furniture and painting are of that color. There are eight large looking-glasses, and some lovely plants. On the walls are portraits, most of them full length, of General Washington, his wife Martha and some of the other United States Presidents. There are three windows at each end of the room.

Our guide took us from here to the green room parlor; the next is the blue room, in which President Cleveland was married. The last one is the red room, where the furniture, the carpets and everything are of that hue. Portraits of Presidents Cleveland, Garfield and others hang on the walls.

Across the street from the White House is the United States Treasury building. The most of these buildings take up one block of ground each. In this one a guide took us into the vaults, and opened some massive iron doors where we had a view through the grating, of perhaps millions of dollars of gold and silver. In the room above, there was a large number of people, mostly ladies, counting paper money at their desks; they ran it through their fingers so swiftly that it seemed that they must make mistakes; but we were told this seldom occurred. Farther back we saw the large wheel that grinds up the bills after they have been redeemed with coin.

The Washington Monument, which we went to see, is five hundred and fifty feet high, and is built in the south west part of the city, near the Potomac River. It is erected on an artificial mound of earth, and shows off to good advantage. The only door or entrance faces east. After going inside we take seats on a bench, and wait for the elevator to return with the passengers who have just gone up, which takes about fifteen or twenty minutes. Inside of the monument, there is barely room for the elevator and some narrow winding stairs, besides the bench we sit upon. The elevator takes its passengers within fifty feet of the top, when they alight and go into a small room with windows on the north, south, east and west; which gives the tourist a view of the city and the country, for miles around. In going up, and coming down, the elevator moves very slowly, therefore we have a chance to read the names of the different states and territories in the Union (Utah included) which are written on the stones they have furnished to help to build the monument. These places of interest in Washington are mostly free to visitors.

Thursday 14th, four more ladies arrived to attend the National Council from Salt Lake City: Mrs. Elmina S. Taylor, President of the Y. L. M. I. A., Minnie J. Snow, Susa Y. Gates, and

Dr. Ellis R. Shipp. They had taken rooms in the Lockwood House, and were anxious that we should go there too, so we could be near them. Consequently we moved the next Saturday, happy to be with our friends from home. Mrs. Belva A. Lockwood has visited Utah twice, and has shown kindness to our people on different occasions. While we were lodgers in her house, we were invited to take dinner with her one afternoon, the occasion being the birthday of her aged mother.

On Sunday I visited a Sunday School of colored children in Mount Carmel Church. I was invited to speak and responded.

Monday, the meeting of the National Council commenced in the Metzeratt Hall, which we attended, wearing our blue badges; these entitled us to seats among the delegates. In the evening went to a reception at the Ebbitt House, Headquarters of the Council and one of the popular hotels in the City. Sister Wells had taken a room there in connection with other prominent ladies. The ladies from Utah, had part of two evenings to deliver their speeches and read their papers.

On the evening of the 20th, Mrs. Elmina S. Taylor presided. Mrs. Minnie J. Snow, read her paper, "The Ethical Side of Woman's Education." Mrs. Susa Young Gates, read her paper, "What is Modern Education doing for American Girls," and also a paper by Mrs. Lillie T. Freeze, "The relative Importance of Preventive to Corrective Work in Moral Reform."

The next evening Mrs. Emmeline B. Wells took the chair. I had the honor of offering the opening prayer. The first reading was, "Heredity and Progressionism," by Dr. Ellis R. Shipp; "The Sixth Sense," paper by Mrs. Sarah M. Kimball was read by Mrs. Marilla Daniels. "The Spirit of Reform Reduced to Practice," by Mrs. L. Lula Greene Richards, was a paper which I should have read, but it was omitted for want of time. Mrs. E. B. Wells had time to read most of her article, "Forty Years in the Valley of the Great Salt Lake."

Washington's birthday, February 22, was a grand affair; companies of soldiers, with bands of music, marched through the city. We saw them in the morning on our way to the Woman's Council at the Metzeratt Hall. The Hall was decorated with flags, and three banners, on which were inscribed suitable mottoes, graced the stage. The old original flag (so they said) was placed beside one of modern date. Among the exercises given, one in particular took my attention, for it reminded me of home. It was by a martial band composed of boys dressed in uniform. Red cap with black tassel, star in front, red waist, blue jacket trimmed with red braid and brass buttons; red knee pants with white leggings, blue sash with red tassel on the end. The captain wore a cap in imitation of solid gold. They went upon the stage and played some enlivening tunes, our country's favorite airs. After which they came down and stood in front, while sixteen girls with flags, also dressed in uniform, took the stage, marching to the music, and going through a drill, "The Balch Salute," keeping the most perfect time. The girl's uniform was a red and white skirt in imitation of the flag; white blouse underwaist, with blue over jacket trimmed with gold braid, black stockings and shoes, caps of red and white ribbon, or cloth. After the drill, the boys went upon the platform again, and a lovely picture was formed, typical of the union of the sexes. Previously small flags had been distributed among the congregation, to be waved at given signals of the salute. I paid for my flag, and brought it home with me.

March 5th we took the car for Mt. Vernon, which is some miles down the Potomac River. This was one of the privileges of my life, to visit the spot where George Washington retired, after the Revolutionary War was over. We saw his large plantation. The old house stands on a rise of ground near the river, just where it was built over a century ago. It is three stories high including the attic, and well preserved, in my opinion; the stairs are very narrow and steep. We went into the room where Washington died, saw the old fashioned bedstead and chairs, with a cushion that Martha Washington made. Going out of the south door, which faces the river, saw a steam-boat come in, landing a few yards below the house, and near the tomb of Washington. I could not help admiring General Washington's choice in selecting a location for his home.

After the council meetings were over, Sister Wells having some visiting and business to attend to, Sister Daniels and myself accepted an invitation of Mrs. Ellen Powell Thompson, who was an acquaintance of Sister Wells and Sister Daniels, to stay at her house while we remained in Washington. We found in her a very dear friend. Her husband also extended a hearty welcome. She spared no pains to have us see as much of the city as possible.

Some of the places we visited of which much might be told, were The Smithsonian Institute, and Museum, The Corcoran Art Gallery, Soldier's Home, Arlington Heights, and the Zoological Gardens, or Park. In this Park, we saw all kinds of animals of land and water, beasts, birds, and reptiles of every description. One thing that interested us very much was the intelligence displayed by two monkeys in their cage. The mother of the younger monkey had died, and the father took the responsibility of watching over his child. When we first went up to the cage, the baby monkey was afraid of us, and ran toward its father, who put his arms around it, and hugged it up to him, as much as to say, "You are safe here."

Sunday, the 11th of March, 1895, we took train for home. On the evening of the 12th arrived at Chicago, where I met with some of my mother's relatives whom I had informed by letter of the time I should be there on my way home. My cousin Edward C. Lovell, his daughter Gertrude, and Miss Smith, another cousin, had come from Elgin, Illinois, to see me, and we had a pleasant visit for a few hours. Here we met Sister Wells, who had taken another route to see some of her friends. The depot where we waited was a fine building, with every convenience for travelers; my cousin ordered dinner for us all.

Mr. Lovell is a lawyer, and prominent in other branches of business; he had visited Utah a few years before, when I met him for the first time.

Before leaving the depot, we went up a few

steps at the east end, where we had a good view of Lake Michigan, whose waters came within a few yards of the building we were in. This might have been the place where the steamboat landed, when my father was moving his family from Massachusetts to Nauvoo. Be that as it may, I remember as a child, when we neared the shore, seeing some Indians sitting on the bank eating crackers and cheese; and noticed what a sensation it created among the passengers. In fact these were the first Indians that I had ever seen. Chicago at that time was not thickly settled, but looked like a vast prairie with a few houses scattered here and there.

After leaving Chicago, nothing requiring particular notice occurred; and in a few days we arrived at our homes in safety.

I felt loth to part with my traveling companions, Sisters Daniels and Wells, who had endeared themselves to me in our constant association with each other for a number of weeks. There was a joyful time in meeting with my family and friends, after an absence of nearly seven weeks; during which time I had not realized one day's sickness. The blessing pronounced upon my head by President John W. Hess, before leaving home, had verily been fulfilled; he said that I should go in peace and return in safety; other blessings had also been pronounced and realized. Oftentimes while in Atlanta and Washington, my heart went out with thankfulness that my lot had been cast among so good a people as those of Farmington, and Davis County; for they had helped me to this enjoyment.

* * *

CHAPTER XVII.

CROWNING EVIDENCES OF LOVE.

An invitation to be present at a special meeting of Primary Officers of all the Stakes of Zion, reached me in my home at Farmington, in the latter part of September, 1897. As the General Conference of the Church of Jesus Christ of Latter-day Saints would open on the 3rd of October, the semi-annual meeting of the Primary

Officers was appointed to be held on the evening of the 4th.

When I received this notice, I felt conscious that the time chosen for the meeting was to do me honor. My sisters and co-laborers were thoughtful of me, and were taking advantage of the circumstance of the early opening of Conference, to hold their meeting on the evening of my birthday. How pleasant it would be, indeed, to meet with so many of my dear sisters who faithfully carry on the Primary work, and hear them talk over their experiences with the children. These were thoughts that came to my mind.

But when, at the appointed hour I entered the 14th Ward Assembly Hall, the place selected for the meeting, I was entirely unprepared for the sight which met my view and the greetings which I received.

Sister Louie B. Felt, with her Counselors and Aids, had planned a most splendid entertainment, and for my benefit!

A profusion of flowers, autumn leaves and boughs, chastely arranged, made the hall appear like an Eden of loveliness. This was all the work of the Salt Lake Stake Board, under the supervision of the Secretary, Mrs. Ella W. Hyde, and Treasurer, Miss Kate Wells, so I was informed. Instead of the business transactions, listening to reports, etc., usual at our officers' meetings, a choice program had been arranged, the whole of which was rendered in a delightful manner. The first was singing by the congregation, "In our lovely Deseret." Prayer was offered by Bishop Geo. H. Taylor. Singing, "Oh my Father!" Address of welcome, President Louie B. Felt. Historical sketch, written by Sister Lillie T. Freeze and read by Sister Maggie F. Basset. As this sketch contains some important statistics, I will insert a portion of it here.

"The amount of faith, courage and persistence and patient determination required by the sisters called to labor in the past can scarcely be estimated, but a deep sense of responsibility and an abiding love for the children of the Saints have inspired heroic efforts in the paths of duty. All honor is due them, especially the pioneer in this movement. What are the results of this devotion for upwards of twenty years? Only the angels can tell, but according to the last annual report made by the General board, which included a report from every Stake in Zion, we can form a little idea of the good being accomplished.

"There are 484 associations, 2,767 officers and 33,659 members. There has been held 13,946 meetings and conferences, representing the spiritual and moral education; 412 entertainments, showing the mental and social; 56 fairs, showing the industrial. The Primary Fair is a very interesting and important feature, originated with Sister Ann Dustin Woolley, of East Bountiful, the first being held in the Association over which she still presides.

"The nature of the exercises can briefly be told from a few statistics. Readings from Church works 24,454; readings and recitations from miscellaneous works 30,259; testimonies borne 17,174; sentiments memorized and stories related 70,207; manuscript papers 294; essays, dialogues, historical sketches and lectures 2,833; musical exercises, vocal and instrumental 13,804.

"Financially hundreds of dollars annually are devoted to charitable purposes, missionary work, traveling expenses and the various enterprises connected with the Church. Thus we see that the opportunities for development are varied, tending to the education of the children spiritually, mentally, morally, physically and socially —the spiritual growth taking the lead."

Song, "Papa, what would you take for me?" by little Emma Taylor. Song composed by Sister Lucy A. Clark; sung by Mrs. Maggie Freeze Bassett, Miss Louie E. Felt, and Messrs. James and Heber Wickens, who were members of the first Primary Association organized in Salt Lake City; Brother Henry A. Tuckett accompanist. This song is the same that appears in the "Surprise" given at Farmington.

At the conclusion of the song, I was presented with a beautiful boquet of roses, by Master Roy Taylor. Recitation, "There never was a grandma half so good!" Master Shirly Jones. Hoop

Drill, by a company of little girls from the west branch of the 15th Ward, led by Miss Gertrude Allen. Recitation, "The motherless Turkeys," Miss Viola Jones. Recitation, "When I am eight," Master Roy Taylor. Reading of Congratulations from President Wilford Woodruff, by Secretary May Anderson. Reading by Brother Joseph H. Felt of a statement from the Geo. Q. Cannon and Sons Publishing Co., announcing that arrangements had been made with them, by the General Board of the Primary Association for the publishing of Sister Aurelia Spencer Rogers' book.

This program was interspersed by addresses from Sisters M. I. Horne, J. S. Richards, E. B. Wells, E. S. Taylor, S. Y. Gates and Helen M. Miller. Brother Barrell, who had organized a Primary Band in early days, also spoke. The speeches were all full of kind and loving words for me, and appreciation of the Primary work.

Delicate refreshments were served, while social chat was carried on, and many of my sister-workers took the opportunity thus afforded of coming to me with cheering smiles and endearing words. At the close of the entertainment, benediction was pronounced by Brother Jesse W. Crosby, President of Panguitch Stake; his wife is also President of the Primaries in that Stake of Zion.

The reading of the statement from the Cannon Publishing Company, was a crowning surprise. It is true the thought had occurred to me that if the Primary Associations knew of my desire to publish a book, they might possibly raise means to assist me in the work. This thought came to my mind in the Fall of 1896, when I mentioned it to Sister Lula Richards. She told me the same idea had presented itself to her mind, and asked and received my permission to lay the matter before the General Primary Board. As to how well and thoroughly the enterprise was being worked up I had not understood until the reading of that paper from the Publishing Co.

It seemed to me then that the Lord had opened up the way for the publishing of my book in the most pleasing and satisfactory way possible. How could the Primary Association have better expressed great love for me than by this ready and cheerful compliance with the request to aid in the accomplishment of this work?

✤ ✤ ✤

CHAPTER XVIII.

CONCLUDING TESTIMONIES—A TRIBUTE BY LULA.

The entertainment described in the preceding chapter, which was given on my sixty-third birthday, finishes this record. Much more that is of interest to me might have been added; but my aim has been to condense the sketches that have been written, that the readers might not weary with their perusal.

I do not wish to have anyone feel that in mentioning the many joyful surprises given me, it has been done boastfully; or with the intention of showing that I have been brought into prominence before the people. But these things are in my life's history; and if the lives of many of my sisters were written, they would be similar to mine in this respect.

By a careful reading of the pages I have written, it will be seen that my blessings have exceeded all my trials. Yet of some of my greatest blessings, I have said but little; perhaps too little, I almost think, when I realize my cause for gratitude. It has always been a source of joy and comfort to me, that the Lord gave me daughters as well as sons. My eldest daughter, Ellen Aurelia, (we call her Ella) has ever been a trusty, faithful helper in her father's household. Lucy Isabella, who came so near dying in her infancy, we have always felt was spared to us for some wise purpose, through the mercies of God. And the youngest, Esther Leone, given to me as if in compensation, after the great trial of my life, has been in my later years, and still is a special consolation and support to me.

In the sad experiences related, the sacrifices which have been made, I sincerely hope there is nothing which might have a tendency to weaken the faith of any Latter-day Saint, or discourage those who may be investigating our religion. And I wish to bear my testimony, that with all that the members of our family have passed through, I have not doubted the truth of the Gospel which I have embraced, and feel that I have great cause to be zealous in testifying that I do know that God lives, and that the Church of Jesus Christ of Latter-day Saints is His true Church.

The one time in my life, which has been referred to, when my children were taken from me by death, and I did almost question the existence of a God, was momentary. The words of my father comforted me, and the seeming doubt when cleared away never returned.

My sister Ellen's testimony has also strengthened my faith in the truth of Mormonism, and it seems to me appropriate to give it here, as it may prove a help to others. She was at a meeting of the Saints, held in a grove west of the Temple in Nauvoo, soon after the death of the Prophet Joseph Smith. The question was under consideration, who should take the Prophet's place in presiding over the Church.

Sidney Rigdon, who had been one of Joseph's Counselors, claimed the right to the position; yet the spirit he manifested was not in accord with the spirit of the Gospel. At this meeting, Brigham Young, who was President of the Quorum of Apostles, arose to speak, when "The Mantle of Joseph" fell upon him, and he was like one transformed; his countenance, voice and form were like those of the late Prophet. Many in the congregation, even children saw this miracle; it satisfied the people, and decided the question who was to be the leader. Sister Ellen occasionally referred to this circumstance, and said whenever she was tried, or felt to doubt any of the principles of the Gospel, this testimony came up before her.

Referring once more to blessings with which I have been favored, I will conclude these sketches with this declaration; friends have ever been raised up to me, as my father said they would be to his children, if they were faithful.

A TRIBUTE.

BY LULA.

"With grateful interest and devoted thought,
   I've read the contents of this volume through;
And found on every page some lesson taught,
   Though grave or light, still valu'ble and true.

High morals, faith sublime and patient trust;
   God's special care for children left alone;
The sure salvation of the faithful just—
   All these, in pleasant style are tersely shown.

And many more; but one is well defined,
   The Primary Work in Zion, its true source;
God's will and wisdom graciously combined,
   To guide our little ones by love—not force.

Mothers in Zion, read, and offer thanks
   To Him who thus one mother's soul impress'd
With the great thought of forming all these ranks,
   Through which our tender darlings are so blest.

Send for the book, love's message pure and sweet,
   That better may be known and understood,
In all the world, where'er our Primaries meet,
   Our children's gentle Prophetess of good."

Errata.

Page ten, third paragraph, instead of Deep River, should read Laybrook.

Fourth paragraph, while living there *two* children were born to them, later on the parents moved to Deep River, the birthplace of the author.

Catherine the eldest, was named for Catherine Read, and the second Catherine for my mother, third paragraph page eleven.

Page forty-three, at the end of second paragraph, for 1836 read 1846.

Page forty-five, sixth line from the bottom, for Sheron read Theron.

Page one hundred and sixty-six, first line in Chapter xviii, for second of January, read first of January, and in third line of same Chapter, for three days read two days.

Page three hundred and thirty-three, first line of last verse, read send forth instead of send for.

www.ingramcontent.com/pod-product-compliance
Lightning Source LLC
Chambersburg PA
CBHW032048220426
43664CB00008B/918